DIALOGUES ON SCHOPENHAUER

DIALOGUES ON SCHOPENHAUER

Finding Our True Nature in a World Adrift

J.P. van Rossum, PhD

Published by Rotheheym Publishing, 2024
Ouderkerk aan de Amstel, The Netherlands

© J.P. van Rossum
jpvanrossum.com

ISBN: 978-90-833528-4-8

Cover image: *Der Chasseur im Walde* by
Caspar David Friedrich (1774–1840)

Original Dutch edition: *De Weg Terug: Schopenhauer voor een
Dolende Wereld* (2022)
Groningen: De Blauwe Tijger

Reality cannot be ignored except at a price; and the longer the ignorance is persisted in, the higher and more terrible becomes the price that must be paid.
Aldous Huxley

We cannot cure the world. Our aim is to get cured of it.
Robert Lemm

Man knows so many things; he does not know himself.
Meister Eckhart

Contents

Preface

Who, or perhaps more fundamentally: what are we? What is our place in the universe and the meaning of life, if any? In the Western world the responses to these profound questions underwent significant changes as the traditional Christian worldview, which for many had become untenable due to scientific discoveries from roughly the 16th century onward, was gradually supplanted by the scientific *Weltanschauung*. This transformation reached its zenith with Charles Darwin, who provided an explanation for existence and the emergence of living beings within a mechanistic universe—a challenge that had vexed philosophers since the time of the ancient Greeks. Since Darwin, modern man has found a new place in the cosmos, as a product of blind chance, devoid of inherent meaning or purpose.

But this new perspective, coupled with the vanishing of Christianity, has presented serious challenges. The erosion of once-secure religious, cultural, and metaphysical foundations has led to feelings of instability, uncertainty, and alienation, in some leading to a sentiment of 'things falling apart', so powerfully expressed in Yeats' poem *The Second Coming*. With others, the new outlook on humanity has bolstered confidence in our ability to improve the world and the human condition, a confidence that, paradoxically, is tied with the collective horrors of the 20th century. Furthermore, the modern worldview often falls short in meeting our existential and spiritual needs, leaving a void that many seek to fill through various means.

While these adverse consequences may not, on their own, offer sufficient grounds to dismiss a philosophical perspective on humanity and the universe, they can serve as a signal that something might be amiss. However, challenges and inconsistencies within this modern outlook raise more reasons for scepticism. A closer look reveals that the scientific worldview, under an apparent consensus, shows signs of strain, particularly at the level of its most fundamental assumptions. For example, in the case of Darwinism, a theory pivotal to this new perspective. Evolution may be a proven fact, but the proposed mechanism behind this process, natural selection, still lacks convincing demonstration. In research that culminated in my PhD thesis in 2014, I discovered and aimed to demonstrate that specific features of sexual reproduction defy the idea that it could have arisen solely through random mutations and natural selection. Problems also persist in physics. The quest to uncover the smallest, indivisible particles and unify the forces of nature—major scientific ambitions— remains unfulfilled even after centuries of effort. The picture painted by quantum physics of the universe is confusing, inconsistent, and thus unconvincing. There is little consensus among physicists on how to interpret the results in this field, with some arguing that they demand a revaluation of the fundamental principles of physics. When we introspect, we encounter inconsistencies in the scientific view of human nature. We hear from many quarters that there is no such thing as free will, with some thinkers even suggesting that the concept of will as such is an illusion. However, this contradicts our own first-hand experiences and deep insights, and should therefore encourage scepticism and prompt us to seek explanations that align more closely with our deepest experiences and beliefs. In fact, I believe that it is precisely at the level of this will where the key to a new paradigm can be found: a worldview that offers a more realistic and veracious perspective on humanity and the world.

It is here where the ideas of Arthur Schopenhauer (1788–1860) come in the picture. The German philosopher lived in an intellectually vibrant era. Science was on the rise and gaining influence, and in its wake, the materialist worldview. During this period, the philosophical groundwork was also laid for ideologies advocating significant improvements in the human condition through radical social or political changes. In short, it was a time that laid the foundation for the Western world as we know it today.

Schopenhauer vehemently questioned these developments. He viewed humanity and the world differently from his contemporaries, seeing them as expressions of the will—a blind, insatiable force at work in everything in the universe. While this message may sound alienating to the modern ear, my work aims to demonstrate that by adopting this perspective, we can gain a much deeper understanding of ourselves and the world, including contemporary societal problems and the scientific challenges mentioned earlier (many of which Schopenhauer predicted). The concept of 'man as will' surprisingly aligns with modern scientific insights as well as with the mystical teachings of East and West. It explains why salvation can only be achieved by the individual and why utopian ideals are destined to fail. Additionally, it offers solutions to long-standing philosophical quandaries, such as the question of free will, the nature of mortality, and the basis of justice in a world often seemingly dominated by its opposite. In short, with Schopenhauer's insights, I believe we can come to understand our true essence, and again find our place and purpose in the universe.

The ideas presented in this book are the result of a profound journey that began after I completed my PhD thesis. My fascination with Schopenhauer's philosophy began in my early twenties but deepened during my PhD research, where I came to realise that naturalism couldn't provide satisfactory answers to fundamental philosophical and scientific questions. This realisation prompted me to embark on a rigorous and systematic analysis of Schopenhauer's philosophical ideas within the context of contemporary scientific discoveries and philosophical theories. My goal was to thoroughly investigate whether Schopenhauer, beyond his brilliance as a writer, was also right in the core of his philosophy. This endeavour took the form of a dialogue between two personas: one - represented by Hugo - embodying Schopenhauer's philosophy, enriched by the insights of more modern thinkers like Aldous Huxley and Arthur Koestler, and the other - represented by Adam - firmly rooted in the science and ideas of our contemporary era, relentlessly posing probing questions and seeking clear answers.

This journey, of which this book can be seen as a travelogue, has left me thoroughly convinced of the value of Schopenhauer's philosophy and its enduring relevance in our modern times. It starts with a meticulous examination of our inner experiences, providing an intimate and first-hand perspective that challenges fundamental conceptions about our true nature. From there, the journey explores the realms of (neuro)psychology, biology, physics, religion, and philosophy, gradually revealing our real nature while also adapting Schopenhauer's philosophy in some areas. As this adventurous voyage reaches its climax, we turn our attention to contemporary societal challenges, delving deeper into how we might navigate our way out of our current challenges.

Before I give Hugo and Adam the floor, I wish to express my gratitude to several individuals whose contributions were pivotal in bringing this work to publication. Serge, Yair, Max, Abel, Derk, Helga, Tineke, Jules, Jan, Tom, Henk-Jan, and Ronald provided invaluable advice, input, edits, and encouragement during the creation of the Dutch edition of this book. After its publication in 2022, I had the privilege of connecting with various inspiring individuals who played a crucial role in the English translation and publication of this work. I extend my heartfelt thanks to Paul Cliteur and Anton Prins for their support and valuable insights.

J.P. van Rossum, March 2024

CHAPTER I

On Knowledge and Understanding

Adam: When we spoke the other day, you talked about the gap between our familiarity with our existence and the complex workings of our bodies. What did you mean by that?

Hugo: Take, for example, seeing, visual perception, and consider the incredible complexity of our eye and the relevant parts of the brain associated with it: light projected onto the retina through the cornea and eye lens, the amount of light meticulously regulated by the sphincter muscles in the iris. The 90 million rod cells and 4.5 million cone cells that convert light into electrical signals that are then transported to the visual cortex, where they are processed into an image... in no way does our seeing betray the enormous physiological complexity that underlies it.

Adam: But this doesn't just apply to seeing.

Hugo: Indeed, this in fact applies to all our experiences, and all other parts of our body that we feel so familiar with. The workings of the physiological and biochemical processes that underpin the most trivial actions are extraordinarily impressive. From the functioning of our muscles to the processes in the cell membrane that guard the delicate chemical composition of our cells, to the anatomical structure of our speech organs: it is of a nature and complexity that bear little relation to how we experience our existence. But despite this ignorance, we have a sense of being in control, of being masters of our existence and bodies. As if our being and functioning need no explanation and is the most natural, obvious thing in the world.

Adam: I don't know if I completely agree with you. I mean, we do have knowledge of the physiology and biochemistry of our bodies, don't we? You make it seem like we are all ignorant about this.

Hugo: You raise an important point. We have knowledge, you are right about that. Indeed, we know an awful lot today about the biological workings of our bodies. But this knowledge will remain of limited value if it does not play a role in our daily lives, if this knowledge is written down in books that we open only occasionally. The essence is to turn this knowledge into an insight, an understanding; that we live through this knowledge as an awareness, so to speak, losing the deceiving familiarity with our existence. And this insight is accompanied by a sense of wonder, what Plato rightly called the starting point of philosophy. It is the wonderment that what we perceive and how we naturally experience life and the world cannot be *the*, or not all of reality. It was in line with this that, in the words of philosopher of science Andrew van Melsen, natural philosophy began when 'Grecian thought was confronted with the fundamental problems which centre around the apparent contradiction between the data of experience and the postulates of reason'.[1]

Adam: I associate wonder mainly with our childhood. Where is the boundary of the universe? Did time start with the Big Bang? Questions of that sort.

Hugo: Perhaps it characterises the philosopher to be able to hold on to that childlike wonder! But not only the physical world, also confrontation with suffering and death, with the imperfection of life, can lead to this wonderment; through the insight 'that there is something wrong about us as we naturally stand', in the words of philosopher William James.[2] Schopenhauer called death the real inspiring genius of philosophy and argued that without death, there would be no philosophy at all.[3] But what is so fascinating, Adam, is that in the history of philosophy, a part of our experience that is so intimately close to us has scarcely led to wonder, and hence to philosophical reflection. And I am talking here about our will. But the more you analyse the expressions of your will and your behaviour, the more you will find that this introspection invalidates many assumptions with far-reaching, indeed fundamental, consequences.

Not only for how we see ourselves, but also for what the real nature of the world is.

Adam: So, the knowledge about ourselves, shared with just about everyone on earth, is wrong? That is quite something to claim.

Hugo: The world that we perceive, that we experience, is not the true world. But that idea is not at all unusual in the world of philosophy. 'We are asleep. Our life is a dream. But sometimes we wake up, just enough to know that we are dreaming', Wittgenstein said. Everyone lives in a dream, and it is the philosopher who tries to wake up.

Adam: But if we are not what we think we are, what are we then, Hugo? What do we encounter when we wake up from the dream?

Hugo: Well, I could tell you here and now what the outcome of this search is and put into words 'what we are'. You can then take in those words and understand them to some extent. And it will not surprise you, given the emphasis on the will, that many of these words relate to Schopenhauer's philosophy. But this knowledge, like the knowledge of the biological basis of our experiences, will be without value if it is not realised, not lived through. The understanding I speak of comes closer to 'seeing' than to 'knowing'. Knowledge is worthless if it remains theoretical and becomes effective only when we realise it as an immediate, intuitive experience. Just as philosophy begins with wonder linked to the insight that the world is not or cannot be as we naturally think it is, so too, philosophical theories are only of value when they reach us as an insight, they sink in as a realisation. We can perhaps understand philosophical works in the sense of learning, analysing, reproducing, and discussing them. This is, in fact, the occupation of academic philosophy. But with that does not automatically come insight into, understanding of that philosophy. At least not with most people, perhaps only with those with exceptionally great powers of imagination. Paradoxical as it may sound, knowledge is not a very effective path to the truth. As the eighth-century Indian philosopher Adi Shankara so aptly put it when he spoke of Brahman, the word for ultimate reality for Vedanta, a school of Hindu philosophy:

A sickness is not cured by uttering the word 'medicine'. You must take the medicine. Liberation does not come by simply saying the word 'Brahman'. Brahman must be actually experienced. Until you allow this apparent universe to dissolve from your consciousness — until you have experienced Brahman — how can you find liberation just by saying the word 'Brahman'? The result is merely a noise.[4]

Or, to quote writer and thinker Aldous Huxley, whom many people know from his books *Brave New World* and *The Doors of Perception* but who has also written a lot about philosophy and spirituality: knowledge is always in concepts and can be communicated through words or other symbols. Insight or understanding (words I use as synonyms) is not conceptual: it is an immediate experience, and it can perhaps be spoken about, but as insight it cannot be passed on through words alone.[5] Sometimes it can be, however, through art, such as music or poetry. In fact, you could call this the essence of art: communication of things that cannot be conveyed by conceptual knowledge. The degree of communicability of insight or understanding is similar to that of emotions, such as sadness, or the feeling of beauty. These feelings can never be conveyed by words or concepts alone; but by reading a novel you can live through the grief of the protagonist; a painting or a poem can convey the feeling of beauty. The same applies to insight. Concepts alone never bring insight, only knowledge. An important implication of this is also that insight cannot be *learned*.

Adam: So it is a fundamental mistake to think that knowledge and insight, or understanding, are the same thing.

Hugo: Exactly. But this misunderstanding, especially today, is widespread. Nowadays knowledge and the mental faculties to acquire and process it — logical thinking, reason, intelligence — are held in very high esteem, while a concept like wisdom, which follows from insight and understanding, sounds old-fashioned and outdated. But knowledge in itself is of limited value. Sometimes because it is trivial and has no direct relation to the essence of our existence. Facts, in other words. A spider has eight legs.

The circumference of the earth is 40,075 kilometres. Those kinds of things. Or because it does not lead to an immediate, direct experience. Take, for example, the fact 'man is mortal'. That is knowledge everyone can acquire. But *realising* that mortality, *living through* it and recognising that this also applies to you personally, that is of a completely different order. And that is true of any philosophical truth. If it is limited to concepts, and not lived through, not accompanied by insight, by understanding, it only is a game of words and hardly of value.

Adam: Knowledge and understanding are different things, and understanding does not come through knowledge alone.

Hugo: And therefore intelligence does not necessarily make people wise and sensible. Indeed, I would venture to say that the power of the human intellect is grossly overestimated and is often rather an obstacle to understanding. As Huxley describes it, human intellect has a strong tendency to oversimplify, overgeneralise and over-abstract, something he calls our intellectual sins, and he sees, among others, as cause of political and religious dogmatism and fanaticism. Moreover, the way people look at and interpret the world is rigid and difficult to adjust, even if facts overwhelmingly contradict these frames of mind. By way of illustration, it took two thousand years for Kepler, Copernicus and Galileo to rediscover what the Greek Aristarchus of Samos already proposed and which offers a much more logical explanation for astronomical observations — that the earth revolves around the sun, and not the other way around. Besides, Adam, gaining insight is not only difficult, it is also not an 'act of will': insight does not come with wanting it. We cannot suddenly decide to gain insight into things. As Huxley put it, 'We cannot make ourselves understand: the most we can do is to foster a state of mind, in which understanding may come to us.' And at the fundamental level of realising our nature, art too is inadequate: it too cannot give us a complete understanding of what we are. No, for the very challenging task of getting to know ourselves, I propose a different, more focused path. The path I propose begins with self-reflection, using our will expressions as a guide. And with insight into our own nature also comes insight into the true nature of the world.

Adam: Metaphysics through introspection?

Hugo: The representatives of Gnosticism, a religious movement from the first few centuries AD, were already saying that knowing yourself at the deepest level means knowing God. Those who know themselves have, at the same time, insight into the essence of the world. As the Arabic gnostic Monoimus put it, 'Abandon the search for God and creation and other matters of a similar sort. Look for him by taking yourself as the starting point.'[6] A search for ourselves through introspection with the will as our guide, critically analysing and extrapolating these insights to phenomena beyond ourselves, can fundamentally change the image of what we are and reveal our true nature, and that of the world. However, note that guarantees are not given. I argue that introspection as a starting point is one of the paths to that understanding, and I hope it will prove to be an effective path for you as well. In any case, it is a lengthy process, requiring focus, self-reflection, and concentration. For what is required is nothing less than letting go of ingrained conceptions about who we are, concepts shared by the lion's share of people and might even be innate, and replacing these concepts with new ideas about the essence of our existence, ideas shared with only a few. The task ahead is to awaken from a world of sleepers. But then again — once that insight is gained, it is an equally daunting challenge to retain it. Like a stone thrown upwards will fall back down, so will our mind, without constant labour, fall back to its natural state.

Adam: So a tough journey, full of challenges. Maybe you can persuade me to start it by giving a hint of what is to come? What are we going to find at the end of this path, Hugo?

Hugo: Then let me tell you this in advance. Our self-image can be described by some elementary concepts: think of body, consciousness, individuality, the self, actions, the will. Furthermore, in our experience, these concepts stand in a certain relation to each other: we are each an individual, the 'I' or ego, being a mixture of body and consciousness. This 'I' has a will and has a body; this will controls the body; we have a brain; et cetera. But introspection will reveal that these concepts are inadequate, and that the relationship we assume between them is incorrect. At the level of our true being, some concepts have no meaning, and new concepts have to be introduced. What we are, and its relation to the brain, the body, the will, the world; even our idea of individuality that we so strongly associate with our identity… all will turn out to be entirely, fundamentally different.

CHAPTER 2

Introspection with the Will as Guidance

Adam: A fascinating prospect, Hugo. I gladly accept the challenge. How and where do we start?

Hugo: Here. With the things I just saw you do, the actions you took while listening to me. I saw your eyes focused on me first, then you looked at your hands. At the same time, you scratched your head, then put your hand on the table. Can you tell me where those actions came from?

Adam: I don't think I understand what you mean. I was the one performing those actions. They came from me. What else should I say about them?

Hugo: That is indeed an important observation. You did those things. They were your actions, you performed them, and you identify with them.

Adam: Yes, I think that goes without saying.

Hugo: But my question then is: *what* made you move your hand, look up, scratch your head? Now you lean back and fold your hands behind your head. What made you decide to do this?

Adam: Um, now that I think about it — that was actually automatic. I mean, it's not like I decided to sit back or anything. There was no conscious decision to do that. Is that what you mean?

Hugo: That is indeed another, equally important observation. Introspection shows that many actions, in fact most of them, happen automatically, that is, involuntarily. You only notice this when you closely analyse yourself. Even if you fixate your mind on a thought, or a particular action, you will notice that other actions are simply set in motion: that you move your head, a foot, or your eyes. Try it out!

These actions befall us, so to speak, but nevertheless, these actions belong to *us*. It is not that someone controls us, like a puppeteer manipulates his puppet. They remain our actions. So we almost never know what our next actions will be, but are never surprised when we have performed them.

Adam: We identify ourselves with our actions, but at the same time these actions are involuntary, in the sense that we do not consciously initiate them. Actions take place automatically. Like so many processes in my body, like breathing, or the heartbeat. I don't see what the problem is.

Hugo: The problem, Adam, is that there is a contradiction in the automatic (i.e., involuntary) occurrence of actions, and the supposed 'I' who is performing them. 'Automatic' implies that you have nothing to do with it, that it is outside of you. But that is not the case. You say yourself — they are your actions, you perform them, and you identify with them. Actions never come as a surprise. We feel very strongly that these actions come from ourselves, and in line with this we also feel fully responsible for them. It is not that there is an automatic pilot that has taken over from us, and we observe our behaviour as detached spectators. On the contrary! None of our actions that take place without corresponding conscious acts of volition (such as deliberate decisions, commitments, or intentions) surprise and amaze us in the slightest. At the same time, actions appear as if from a dark depth, bubbling up from a source we cannot see.

Adam: But this is not new at all, Hugo. Many modern scientists and scholars, such as the philosopher Sam Harris, would agree that most of the actions we perform are not triggered by conscious acts of volition at all, but take place involuntarily and automatically.[7] This is because neurological processes, and not our will, are behind our actions.

Hugo: Be a bit more specific.

Adam: For example, there is the view that behaviour should be primarily seen as stimulus-response associations: the brain receives a stimulus — for example, a visual impression, or pain or hunger — and based on these stimuli a response takes place, such as looking for food, or pulling your hand away from a flame.[8] Several types of these associations exist in the brain. Many of them are unconscious, as in the case of the automatic motor response or reflexes. Sometimes these reflexes are instinctive, in other cases the result of training, such as in the case of playing a musical instrument or playing a ball sport. For instance, after many hundreds of hours of training, your brain learns and stores how to hit a racket against a ball with a certain speed, spin, and direction to get it to a desired spot. This is something psychologists call procedural memory. But even trivial actions, like doing the dishes or putting on your clothes, are more or less automatic actions stored in the brain. Other parts of the brain can establish stimulus-response associations between internal stimuli, such as hunger or fear (mediated by the release of hormones) and certain actions, such as eating or fleeing. In this way, emotions, as well as things like social contexts, rewards, and punishments, play a role in our behaviour. Other associations between stimuli and actions occur at long intervals, and others are triggered by information that never reaches our consciousness, but subconsciously affects our actions. In short, many different parts of our brain play a role in our actions, each part responsible for a particular stimulus-response association. Which response to a stimulus is the strongest ultimately determines a person's behaviour.

Hugo: But we feel that actions come from our free will.

Adam: That is a trick of our brains, a cognitive and emotional illusion. One theory is that this illusion originated as a metaphor for being able to predict the behaviour of others. This assuming that supposed 'intentions' are better equipped to serve as a source of prediction than neurological stimulus-response associations (and the ability of predicting behaviour being a valuable trait in evolutionary terms of course). Somewhere in evolution, humans started applying these terms to themselves as well, creating the illusion that our will is actually the cause of behaviour.[9]

Hugo: That last one doesn't sound very convincing, do you think?

Adam: Reality has often turned out to be stranger than we previously thought. Do you have a better solution then?

Hugo: Yes, there is a much more elegant way out of the paradox between the automatic nature of our actions and our identification with them, because that is the issue before us. And that is the realisation that this paradox is an outgrowth of wrong assumptions.

Adam: And those are…?

Hugo: Assumptions about what the 'I' is.

Adam: The self is not what we think it is?

Hugo: Indeed. As an aside, it is very difficult to determine exactly what we think we are, what that 'I' is. I am sure we will come back to that later, but in any case, it is clear that we associate ourselves to a large extent with consciousness, with knowing. Agreed?

Adam: I would concur, yes. We are above all conscious, thinking beings, knowing individuals.

Hugo: But that implies that we must also relate the origin of our actions to this conscious self. Decisions, actions are 'our' actions. And since 'we' are conscious, knowing individuals, actions are our actions insofar as the conscious, knowing self was involved in them.

Adam: But wait, they are, aren't they? I mean, I'm aware that I just lifted my eyes, that I moved my foot, that I folded my hands behind my head?

Hugo: That's right. Although this is only to a certain extent, because often we are not even aware of our actions. Just think of all the movements you make while performing trivial activities, such as going for a walk. Many of them remain unconscious if you don't pay attention to them. But the issue here is not whether we are aware of the actions, but whether we *have consciously initiated* these actions. Whether they were voluntary, in other words. Our idea of ourselves makes us assume that conscious acts of volition underlie the majority of them. Actions are willed, and willing is something we associate with intentionality, with consciousness. This idea is found in common descriptions of the will. According to Wikipedia, for example, the will is 'the cognitive process by which an individual decides on and commits to a particular course of action.' The will is seen as an individual's ability to proceed to an action through conscious acts of volition; as the capacity of a person to move from a thought or set of thoughts (such as commitments or decisions) to an action. But, as we saw, most actions are involuntary, that is, are not preceded by conscious processes at all!

Adam: But these actions *can* be initiated by conscious decisions. I mean, I can now decide to move my hand, or blink my eyes.

Hugo: That's an important point. In reality, most of our actions, actions that we identify ourselves with, are not preceded by conscious decisions. But they can often be made voluntary. You are able to decide to move your arm, turn your head, or hold your breath. But nevertheless, most of your actions are involuntary, that is, they are not preceded by thoughts, by conscious acts of volition. Analyse yourself and you will realise this yourself.

Adam: So there are voluntary actions and involuntary actions. Some of the latter can be made voluntary. Then you have conscious processes and unconscious processes, which seems to be a different category. Right?

Hugo: Indeed. Opposed to conscious processes are unconscious processes; terms that at first glance seem clear. Conscious processes are processes like cycling, eating, and talking. Unconscious processes include things like the beating of the heart, digestion, and all kinds of biochemical processes. However, a deeper analysis shows that this dividing line is not so clear-cut and that unconscious processes can sometimes be made conscious, and vice versa. Take breathing. It can happen automatically, meaning we don't think about it. In fact, this is the case most of the time. How often do we breathe without being aware of it? Probably more than 99.99% of the time. But we can make ourselves aware of it. And *subsequently* these processes can be influenced by conscious acts of volition, i.e., made voluntary. After all, we can decide to breathe faster or slower, or even to hold our breath altogether. Another example is the blinking of the eyes. This generally takes place unconsciously, but we can make ourselves aware of the blinking and then also trigger it through conscious acts of volition. Then there are processes that are completely unconscious and also cannot be made voluntary, such as the change in pupil size due to changing light intensity, or the beating of the heart.

Adam: So the dividing line between conscious and unconscious processes is not sharp.

Hugo: Right. Some processes are indisputably unconscious, cannot be made conscious, and therefore not influenced by conscious acts of volition. Think of cellular processes, the heartbeat, the functioning of organs. Other unconscious processes can enter consciousness, and then be modified by conscious expressions of our will. Like breathing. Then you have actions triggered partly by conscious acts of volition, after which the autopilot takes over. For example, I decide to go cycling and get on the bike, and the cycling then takes place without further conscious acts of volition. We can question whether this type of process can therefore still be called conscious: yes, I am aware of the fact that I am cycling the whole time I am on a bicycle, but I am not aware of the actions that accompany it, such as the pedalling, or the complex movements that cause balance to be maintained. And then there are the voluntary actions triggered by expressions of our conscious will. These, as we have seen, are far in the minority. Indeed, most actions and processes will be set in motion without any such conscious decisions.

Adam: Some processes are totally unconscious; some can be made conscious. And among the latter, only a minority are actually triggered by conscious acts of volition.

Hugo: Exactly. And now an important point, Adam. As soon as our actions enter our consciousness, we automatically experience them as 'willed'. Whether actions were voluntary or involuntary, or actions or processes were initially unconscious but later entered our consciousness: we experience them, apart from automatic reflexes such as sneezing or coughing, as willed actions, as actions stemming from our will. We might as well have initiated these actions by conscious decisions. So, we need to see our will as something much larger, more comprehensive than what it is according to the common definition (that is, as the cognitive process by which an individual decides on and commits to a particular course of action). Our will is active in both conscious and unconscious processes. Consciousness, then, should be seen as something that occasionally shines a light on it, but more often does not. But in all cases, it is *our* will.

Adam: But what is this will then, Hugo? If it is not man's conscious ability to decide on a course of action, then what is the will?

Hugo: My aim here and now is not to give a complete definition of the will. Indeed, that won't prove to be a simple task. What I am referring to now when I talk about the will is that which makes us act, makes us move, and with which we then identify very strongly. And is sometimes accompanied by a degree of consciousness, but often not.

Adam: But is this really the case? Is the will really that which makes us act, makes us move? I mean, sometimes I move against my will. Imagine a man walking with his hands behind his back to an execution site to be shot. You can't say that this person steps to his death of his own will, can you?

Hugo: Yes, that which makes the condemned person walk to the firing squad is indeed his will. But we should not confuse *willing something* with *something stemming from our free will*. You can rightly say that this person is not walking to the firing squad voluntarily, voluntarily in the meaning of coming out his free will. And by that, I mean that without the gun at his back, he would not be walking towards his death. But given the situation, namely the choice between being dragged to the spot by force, or a certain, quick death by a shower of bullets without that force, he chooses the latter. You may call that paradoxical, or irrational, but it is still an expression of his will, a choice he makes. You find the same irrationality, though to a lesser extent, in other actions too. Consider someone lighting up a cigarette: here the immediate gratification of the nicotine is chosen over the risk of an early death and diseases in the longer term.

Adam: That distinction between action out of one's will and acting out of one's *free* will in this specific meaning, is interesting. I didn't make that before.

Hugo: Suppose the convict is dragged to the firing squad, then he no longer acts of his own will. But all actions initiated by a person himself, there is the will in action. No matter how irrational they may be.

Adam: But then there is something else: in my opinion, you link the will too much to actions, movements. Although you convincingly suggest that all movements are willed (although not always out of one's free will in the definition above), the will can also occur without movements, actions. For example, I can want something in my mind:

a new car, going to the bakery to buy bread this afternoon, et cetera. Or *not* want something. To use the firing squad as an example — I don't want to be shot.

Hugo: That is absolutely right. The will can also manifest itself in a wish, desire, or fear. But again, my aim here and now is not to give a comprehensive definition of the will. My point is only that what makes us move and act is the will — even in involuntary actions — although the will can also manifest itself in other ways. And then that popular assumptions about this will are wrong. The will is not merely the cognitive process by which an individual decides on and commits to a particular course of action. The will, in the context of what makes us act and with which we identify so strongly, is in most cases not mediated by consciousness.

Adam: Okay, so ignoring the complete definition of the will for now, the point you are making is that sometimes our will is set in motion by conscious processes (the so-called voluntary actions), but more often it is not.

Hugo: Right. And that overturns the popular definition of the will.

Adam: Willing is primary, and being aware of this willing is secondary?

Hugo: You could indeed put it that way. We have to tilt the image of our will: it is not rooted in our knowing, it is not the result of it. This will is autonomous, independent of knowing. Our consciousness sometimes shines a light on it, we sometimes become aware of our will, but the will, our will, is independent of the awareness of it. And that is a fundamental shift in how we view the will. And equally fundamental are the implications that this has for the image of what we are. Since we identify ourselves with all our expressions of our will, but the conscious self plays a very limited role in it, what we are is much less associated with this conscious self than we think.

Adam: We are not so much conscious, thinking, knowing individuals, as I thought earlier, but our being, on the contrary, is very much associated with this willing.

Hugo: That is indeed my point.

Adam: That is certainly a fundamental shift. It is actually the opposite of what Harris and similar thinkers claim: the will is not an illusion, as they argue, what we are is instead very strongly linked to that will.

Hugo: Exactly. By the way, there is another idea about the functioning of the will that, with the observation that our will usually operates involuntarily, is refuted. This is the notion that there is a causal relationship between our will decisions and our actions, and that there would thereby exist a clear distinction between mental processes of the will on the one hand, and physiological processes that occur as a consequence of those on the other. It is the idea that we as conscious beings, through voluntary actions, control the body as we would control a car or any other machine; the knowing and thinking self behind the wheel, the self as driver and master of the body. For we saw that, in most cases, the knowing and thinking self — the entity we associate with our being — is not involved in processes of the will at all, and so there is no causal relationship between processes of volition, and the triggering of the body as a result of these processes, thus making the supposed distinction between the two — the self and the body — unclear.

Adam: The relationship between the will and the bodily processes triggered by this will is not clear?

Hugo: At least not comprehensible in the usual way. But even in those cases where actions *are* preceded by conscious processes, where we consciously want something and the action follows from those acts of volition, the relationship between will and action is still unfathomable. As Aldous Huxley also notes in his essay 'Who Are We?':

> I say, I wish to raise my hand. Well, I raise it. But who raises it? Who is the 'I' who raises my hand? Certainly it is not exclusively the 'I' who is standing here talking, the 'I' who signs the checks and has a history behind him, because I do not have the faintest idea how my hand was raised. All I know is that I expressed a wish for my hand to be raised, whereupon something within myself went to work, pulled the switches of a most elaborate nervous system, and made thirty or forty muscles — some of which contract and others relax at the same instant — function in perfect harmony so as to

produce this extremely simple gesture. And of course, when we ask ourselves, how does my heart beat? how do we breathe? how do I digest my food? — we do not have the faintest idea.[10]

Adam: I am beginning to see it. Even if actions are voluntary — and these cases, contrary to the popular idea, are by far the minority — it is still a mystery how the will actually operates, and what the connection is between these acts of volition and actions, actions with their own unconscious processes and mechanisms, such as the complex workings of muscles. This reminds me of a saying by the twentieth-century writer Arthur Koestler: everyone can ride a bicycle, but no one knows how it works...

Hugo: Exactly! What, Adam, is our actual involvement in these processes, whereby 'our', by 'we', we mean the conscious self? You are listening to me now. What is actually happening here? Air vibrations produced by my vocal cords make your eardrum vibrate; three ossicles amplify these vibrations and transmit them to the so-called oval window, which then transmits these vibrations to the fluid in the cochlea. Next, hair cells, some 30,000 in total, on the organ of Corti are set in motion by vibrations from the basilar membrane, so ingeniously able to distinguish pitch; through their bending, the hair cells convert mechanical energy into electrical energy that is transmitted to the central nervous system via the auditory nerve. This is happening while you are listening to me right now! And what do you, as a conscious I, have to do with this? With these processes during hearing, with the development of these organs during embryonic development, with their evolutionary development? Nothing!

Adam: The 'I' hears, but the 'I' does not know how this hearing works. The self here is nothing more than a witness to the representation, whether it is image or sound. But how this performance comes about is therefore totally independent of this 'I'.

Hugo: That's exactly it. So, it's not just that the relationship between the self and the will is fundamentally different from what we think. Representations, perceptions of this self are based on processes and structures in which it has no part at all, which totally bypass this self. Think of a new-born baby. The moment it leaves its mother's womb, its actions begin immediately: the moving of its limbs, squawking, and seeking its mother's breast. How can you reconcile this with the idea of a prominent role of the conscious self? If our traditional image of ourselves as master and director of the body were correct, every new-born would look out into the world utterly confused and puzzled, wondering where on earth it has ended up!

Adam: You have a point there.

Hugo: But there is more, Adam. Another part of the misconception of the relationship between the self and the will lies in the idea that our will finds its ground in the objects to which this will is directed. The knowing or thinking self wants this or that because those things *are* desirable. I want to have children because it *is* intrinsically nice to have children. I am attracted to this woman because she *is* beautiful. In doing so, we absolutise, objectify the value we assign to objects.

Adam: Wait, now you're going too far, Hugo. We do know for sure that many of these things are relative. After all, they are the products of evolution. For example, we understand that we evolved to find women with certain characteristics attractive because they guarantee the best offspring. Or to like certain foods because they have high nutritional value. Everything, we know since Darwin, is the product of evolutionary mechanisms, and therefore relative.

Hugo: That is book knowledge, Adam. But this knowledge, this science does not penetrate our immediate consciousness, nor does it affect our daily behaviour. This knowledge has not sunk in as an understanding, as an insight. The example you just gave about evolution remains abstract knowledge. I mean, has understanding that evolutionary processes underlie what we find attractive changed your behaviour? Did it affect your 'finding women beautiful', did it make you experience women less attractive? Because that is the effect that understanding the background, the basis of finding things attractive, will have. When you realise, when you understand that those beautiful breasts, those wide hips, actually indicate 'the potential of a strong offspring', then you no longer see them as beautiful, as attractive. Then the spell breaks! Again, remember the essential difference between knowledge and understanding. We still experience things as beautiful, attractive, and desirable, and our expressions of the will are still assumed to be based on the supposed intrinsic value of the objects at which this will is directed. Incidentally, this idea — we pursue things because they are objectively desirable — has led us to interpret the activities of animals in a fundamentally different way from our own. After all, we see nothing desirable in mating with a mouse, or spinning a web, or laying eggs in larvae or pupae of insects as the parasitic wasp does. Hence, animals are not attributed a will like humans but are said to be guided by instinct, with their actions being seen as a programmed automatism, as a fixed pattern of behaviour as a response to stimuli.

Adam: Instinct — I had to think of the term when you talked about involuntary actions, actions not initiated by conscious acts of volition.

Hugo: But if we define instinct as an automatic behaviour, by actions not mediated by a conscious self, then humans can equally be said to be guided by instinct in the vast majority of cases: with them, too, most actions are not preceded by conscious decisions!

Adam: So perhaps our will operates in us in the same way as that in animals.

Hugo: That is indeed my point. Even in humans, most actions, most expressions of the will take place without the involvement of consciousness. Besides, there is nothing objectively 'beautiful' or 'tasteful' or 'nice' about those things we pursue, any more than they are with other organisms. Things are beautiful, tasteful, and nice in the context of the organisms we are, and the circumstances for which we are adapted.

Adam: With which the distinction between me and a mouse, or a spider, suddenly becomes a lot smaller… so gradually, the image we have of our will and ourselves is getting pretty messed up indeed!

Hugo: Are we really what we think we are when our assumptions about something as fundamental as our will turn out to be inconsistent with reality? Let me recap the popular, mainstream picture we have of ourselves: we, as thinking and knowing entities, have the conscious ability to move from a thought to an action, and as a result strive for pursuable things, such as starting a family, eating good food, et cetera. Animals, however, are not equipped for thinking and knowing, and their actions must therefore be interpreted fundamentally differently, also because their will is directed towards things that cannot reasonably be seen by us as worthy of pursuit. But we have established first of all that introspection unmistakably shows that by far most of our actions are involuntary, in the sense that there are no conscious acts of volition of the 'thinking and knowing I' involved at all. Nevertheless — Oh, wonder! — these actions are always experienced as completely one's own. And this also refutes the idea that decisions of this 'I' precede these actions. The fact that actions occur 'naturally', that is, seemingly automatically, where we recognise our will but cannot see a causal link in time between will and action, means that the distinction between what we see as ourselves — the knowing and thinking self — and the body cannot be made clearly. Whereby, incidentally, that link between will expression and action itself, as Huxley aptly wrote, was always to remain a mystery even in the original, erroneous conception of the will. In addition, we must conclude that there is no ground for assuming that there is anything intrinsically beautiful or valuable about those things we pursue, any more than they are in other organisms we observe, so that the will in humans does not operate substantially differently from that in animals.

Adam: All in all, this is pretty overwhelming, Hugo. A lot of information to process…

Hugo: Speaking of processing, let me give another example of a physiological process that illustrates my point: digestion. Here too we see the typical mixture of unconscious and conscious processes including all gradations between the two, with the latter actually only playing a role at the beginning and at the end of the process and being by far in the minority. It starts with ingesting food, food that through smell, colour and taste is selected and introduced into the oral cavity. And there the processes begin that can be made voluntary but are mostly involuntary: the chewing by which the food is finely ground, and the action of the tongue that plays an important role in this chewing process as well as in preparing food chunks to be swallowed. Yes, the tongue can be controlled by conscious acts of volition — here,

I stick out my tongue — but the movements of the tongue during chewing take place automatically and are so sophisticated that they are hardly reproducible by conscious acts of volition — just analyse its action while eating! Then swallowing, which, although it can be consciously initiated, usually is not. And how complex and multifaceted are the unconscious processes that take place alongside and especially afterwards! The saliva produced by the salivary glands, saliva that makes food mushy and contains enzymes that initiate digestion. The automatic closure of the nasal cavity by the uvula and the trachea by the epiglottis — and here we really have arrived at the unconscious processes. And how ingenious these processes are: transporting food chunks to the stomach via squeezing — peristaltic — movements of the oesophagus, contracting the stomach, adding hydrochloric acid, enzymes, bile, absorbing nutrients in the small intestine, extracting water and digesting remaining plant material in the large intestine... Oh yes, and conscious processes start playing a role again at — literally — the end of the tunnel, when the stool has to be discharged. So here again the mixture of conscious and unconscious processes, with the former thus clearly in the minority, and the really sophisticated work taking place in the unconscious. You see, Adam, after all we have discussed, we cannot possibly still see ourselves as drivers, as conductors of our bodies, can we? Let alone talk about 'our' body. No — the role of the self is modest, part of a larger, highly sophisticated, and complex system, and it is limited to a small aspect of the whole process.

Adam: Whatever we are, driver, master of our bodies we are not in any case.

Hugo: Exactly. As Schopenhauer put it, in line with what you noted earlier: it is a fundamental error to associate our nature primarily with knowing or thinking, and only as a consequence of this, secondarily and derivatively, as willing.[11] The fact that most expressions of the will are involuntary — something we have demonstrated conclusively through introspection, and I recommend that you continue to do so in order to hold on to this important insight — combined with our identification with these actions, immediately demonstrates the fallacy of this idea. Therefore, the importance of these conclusions

— obtained first-hand through introspection — cannot be over-stated. It forces us to interpret our being in a different way.

Adam: We should then see ourselves primarily as willing beings? We *are* the will, as Schopenhauer argued, is that what you're getting at? Sorry, but that's still a bridge too far for me. And to be fair, you still haven't shown why Harris and similar thinkers can't simply be right. Their contention that only neurological processes are behind our actions, and that the idea that the will plays a role in this is a cognitive and emotional illusion, has not been refuted by your story.

Hugo: But then, we are far from finished. Let's go another layer deeper, Adam. We concluded earlier that we saw ourselves primarily as thinking, conscious, knowing individuals.

Adam: Which we turned out not to be.

Hugo: But that's not my point now. My question is: what is this 'I'? And by this I mean: what is this self on an ontological level? What are we?

Adam: Um... well, we discussed that, right? An individual. Adam, or Hugo, or Anne. A person. A conscious individual.

Hugo: Okay, a conscious individual, a person. But that's still too vague for me. Try to be more precise.

Adam: I believe I understand what you are getting at. Here then: the self is an individual consciousness, a carrier of experiences? The self is the person who thinks, perceives, feels.

Hugo: That is certainly an important aspect of what you are. The self is the person who thinks, perceives, feels. But your body then? You look in the mirror or you see yourself in a photo, that's you too, isn't it...?

Adam: Yes, that's right. I am also the person I see in the mirror. A body: an entity in time and space, in addition to a consciousness, a carrier of experiences. Well then, I am a combination of body and consciousness?

Hugo: This description is undoubtedly closer to the intuitive sense of what we are. We look in the mirror and see something there that we associate with ourselves. At the same time, we experience ourselves as conscious individuals, as subjects. And then there is the will.

You are also a willing individual, right? That too must have a place in your description.

Adam: Um, yes, that should also be added...

Hugo: But do you realise what we are exposing here? We all have an intuitive sense of ourselves: thinking entities, individuals who take actions based on rational decisions, persons we recognise in the mirror or in photographs, et cetera. But this is not accompanied by a consistent and clear concept of what we actually are, on an ontological level. This is my first important point: despite not knowing what we truly are, we seem surprisingly comfortable with this ambiguity. My second point is that attempting to define our essence proves to be an immensely challenging task. Rest assured, we're not alone in grappling with this issue. I once read that Augustine compared the 'self' to an abyss; the more you think about it and the deeper you search for its essence, the more mysterious it becomes. Or as Huxley said, 'The moment we begin thinking about it in detail, we find ourselves confronted with all kinds of extremely difficult, unanswered, and maybe unanswerable questions...'[12]

Adam: It is indeed striking that our intuition of what we are is not easy to articulate, although in our daily lives this never leads to identity problems. There is no doubt we feel we are an individual, while it is not easy to define exactly what that is. A combination of body, individual consciousness and will, but what exactly that remains very difficult to describe.

Hugo: But are you aware of the fundamental implications of what you say there, Adam? A little reflection shows that we hardly know anything about the most basic, the most fundamental aspect of existence — ourselves! Knowledge about our nature, about what we are, is not given to us in our natural state. We live without truly knowing who or what we are, and how astonishing this realisation is! When we then attempt to articulate our ontological essence, we often find ourselves grasping at vague notions such as 'individual,' 'self,' or a combination of body and mind. Yet, upon introspection, we discover that descriptions of ourselves as self-directing, autonomous entities, and analogies likening us to drivers of our bodies, fall short and prove to be erroneous. This self is much smaller, plays a much more modest role. As Huxley wrote: 'We as we think of ourselves are a very small part even of the physiological and subconscious life immediately available to us.'[13] But what we are is bigger than this self, bigger than a combination of consciousness and body. At the very least, it is much more intertwined with the rest of the organism, which is demonstrated by the intimate connection we feel with our will: a will that is often unconscious, but every time it makes itself known, is experienced again as familiar and as our own. But equally important and fundamental is the notion that being and knowledge about that being are two different, disconnected things. That in our natural state we do not know what we are is also an insight that — regardless of what we eventually turn out to be — completely undermines assumptions about our existence.

Adam: That is indeed a wondrous thing. It is not only that we have refuted the image of ourselves as leading, autonomous entities, but also, and perhaps more fundamentally, as knowing beings. We live our lives without knowing what we are, and we don't even realise that!

Hugo: Indeed, the most wonderful thing about all this is that without realising it, we don't know what we are. We accept life as a given, and do not question it further. We see the wondrous in the stars but overlook the wondrous in ourselves.

Adam: Just as an animal accepts life as it presents itself, just as a cat does not wonder what or who it is, yes does not even recognise itself in the mirror but nevertheless lives its life without being plagued by existential questions: that is how most people live their lives.

Hugo: A cat looks in the mirror and does not recognise its reflection — we look in the mirror and think we see ourselves. But in fact, we are as ignorant about ourselves as that cat. We saw that a lot of assumptions about our self were wrong. And that, on closer inspection, we couldn't even put this 'self' into words. No, our true nature is not this ego, this self. This illusion we have dispelled; from this sleep we have awakened. Let us then, guided by will, continue our path in search of what we really are.

CHAPTER 3

On Materialism

Adam: Back to the will then. At the very least, you made me realise that this will plays an important role in what we are. But Schopenhauer went even further. According to him, we *are* that will?

Hugo: On the face of it, a bizarre statement, isn't it? But it's an assumption that solves the curious conundrum that we have encountered a couple of times: that although the expressions of our will are seldom initiated by conscious processes, by thoughts, this will is always fully experienced as our own. According to Schopenhauer, we feel so intimately connected with this will because it constitutes man's 'inner, true and indestructible nature'.[14] This makes it understandable how the necessity and automaticity of the expressions of our will can be reconciled with the sense of responsibility for these actions.

Adam: You already announced that the image we have of ourselves would change profoundly, but this does go quite far. We are our will, I am my will? What does that mean? This so much goes against intuition that I would like to ask you a counter-question: what does that mean, then, to 'be' something? Is there an objective criterion by which I can determine what I am? Subject, will, body? What makes something 'be', and does not make it a purely subjective, arbitrary assumption?

Hugo: An interesting point, but first let's turn it around. Let's assume that we are a combination of subject and body, regardless of exactly what the relationship between the two is. With this, we are first and foremost an individual, right?

Adam: With that, I agree.

Hugo: Then let's look at the fundamental problems we run into with that assumption. First of all, the following. If we identify ourselves as an individual, then at some point we were thrown into this world, *geworfen* as Heidegger called it, created out of nothing only to disappear from it after a while into eternal nothingness. A brief flash of existence between an infinite non-existence before and after. And what makes this existence even stranger is that it seems to be based on insanely great coincidence. After all, if my mother had not met my father at just that moment in just that place (and their parents' parents, and that *ad infinitum*), and had that sperm cell not fertilised that egg out of all those hundreds of millions of sperm cells that were released during ejaculation, and add to that all the coincidences that were at the basis of exactly my conception, we would not have been born at all, and would never have existed, right?

Adam: You have a point there. My existence seems to depend on exactly these parents, yes, on exactly that sperm cell and that egg. With any other combination, a different person would have been born.

Hugo: But that makes our existence totally contingent. Something that might as well not have existed. Indeed, something that had an incredibly small chance of ever coming into being. A miracle, but also a miracle that can be undone just like that and with great randomness. So why was it precisely we who were born? This is something associated with such an improbably small chance that you could call it a paradox.

Adam: If the essence of our existence is contained in the individual, then this existence is indeed based on an insanely great coincidence.

Hugo: That is indeed the crux. Therefore, this paradox disappears if you do not consider the individual as the essence of our existence, but as something secondary. Or, in other words, it arises because we see ourselves as individuals. And this paradox thus dissolves if we consider the individual not as our true being, but as a form, or phenomenon, of something else, something more fundamental whose existence does not depend on mere chance. Our 'being' can be compared in this way to the waves in the sea: just as the wave is a temporary manifestation of something larger — the sea — so too are we the temporary manifestation of something greater. When a wave arises, we also do not marvel at the emergence of precisely that wave with that particular form. Because we put the essence not in the wave, but in the seawater from which that form was created.

Adam: So you claim that this mystery of our existence disappears when we see ourselves as the modification of something that already existed, not as something unique that has been created.

Hugo: Our being is 'similar to the sun, which seems to set only before our earthly eyes, but which really never sets; it shines on incessantly', as Goethe beautifully put it.[15] But let me address another fundamental problem involved in associating our being with the individual, a problem which is solved by Schopenhauer's thesis that we are the will. We see in both humans and animals that many expressions of the will are not in the interest of the individual. A mother sacrificing herself for her young, sterile insects grooming the queen of a colony: how do we explain this?

Adam: In animals, this is explained by the concept of instinct: a pre-programmed, fixed pattern of behaviour. And in humans...

Hugo: ... by the notion that these things are inherently worthwhile to pursue, right? As we just discussed: people want children because it is simply nice to have children, and a mother protects her offspring with her life because children are the most valuable thing in the world. But we concluded that there is no reason to believe that these things are objectively valuable. Yet it is important to realise that this paradox — individuals pursuing things that are not in the interest of the individual itself — stems primarily from the assumption that these will expressions arise from an individual, leading to the expectation that they would then also be in the individual's interest. But if our true identity lies not in the individual, but in something that transcends it, then this problem disappears! So again, this paradox has its origin in false assumptions, namely that we are individuals.

Adam: I see your point, Hugo, although evolutionary theory has its own explanation for this, of course.

Hugo: We will come back to the theory of evolution later. But first yet another problem that arises with seeing ourselves as individuals.

We discussed earlier that death is the muse of philosophy, just as it is, incidentally, for religion. In my view, this relates not only to the fear of death, but also to a deep, unwavering sense that we are immortal, or at least that an essential part of ourselves is. It is the inner conviction that existence cannot end with death. This widespread and persistent intuition of immortality in its various forms serves as a compelling indication of its validity.

Adam: Hang on, Hugo. Since when is being widespread an indication of validity? Arthur Koestler, whom I referred to earlier, saw it differently. According to him, the belief in life after death is the result of a struggle between reason on one side, and instinct and feeling on the other, and thus an expression of a discord in the human mind, a theme he wrote a lot about.[16] Reason knows that life is ending, but feeling and instinct, located in more primitive brain parts that have not yet been sufficiently outstripped by the newer parts of the brain where reason resides, cannot accept this. Hence the battle between faith and reason. With the result that the thinking half of the mind has to provide rationalisations in order to assuage the older parts' fear of emptiness and death. And so this belief is translated into, for modern man, unsatisfactory dogmas, such as a heaven where we go after death, the idea of reincarnation, or the survival in the form of spirits among primitive peoples.

Hugo: An interesting and original theory, no doubt. But although I am an admirer of Koestler, I disagree with him here. I place greater value on our sense of immortality and see it not so much as an instinct, but as a deep insight, a metaphysical conviction. I find Schopenhauer on my side here. He speaks of a deep consciousness about the immortality of our nature, which prevents the abstract and theoretical certainty of our death from penetrating into actual consciousness.[17] And more importantly, I see the artificiality of dogma around immortality that makes it so unsatisfying primarily as a result of trying to link immortality to the individual, the self, that with which we wrongly associate our existence. The individual arguably disappears with death, and you need to be quite inventive to make it survive. Hence the idea of heaven, or reincarnation, or the idea of spirits, in which we would live on after death. But the assumption that we are the will solves this problem all at once! The individual dies, there is no doubt about that. So if we were this individual, this 'I', then there is no life after death. But if we are not the individual but the will, the will that is eternal, the will that resides in me but also in you, in fact in everything, then death does not affect us. The problem of mortality, as we should call it, exists because we falsely identify our existence with the individual. With the will as our true being, we have found our immortality! The individual, on the other hand, is a temporary manifestation, but our true being exists everywhere and always, in all beings.

Adam: This sounds logical and consistent, I must admit. But none of this convinces me yet of the idea that I should see myself as will. After all, you still haven't shown that your explanation is more logical, or even more elegant, than that of Sam Harris and likeminded modern scientists and philosophers. They would agree that we are not what we intuitively think we are. We are first and foremost a biological phenomenon. In fact, we are an organ, just as the heart or the liver is: a part of the body with a clear role and function within the whole. Our being *is* consciousness; we are our brain, and the brain, as an organ, must be considered primarily in its biological context. You said it yourself when talking about digestion: consciousness has a clear role in this process: searching for food, testing the suitability of this food based on smell, colour, and taste. And of course putting this food into the digestive tract, after which 'our' task is completed and unconscious processes after swallowing soon take over. And consciousness is switched on again at the other end of the process when faeces and urine are discharged. Consciousness, in other words, is an organ like any other, with a distinct role and function within the biological functioning of the — physical — body. A consciousness sprung from the brain. And the brain is made up of matter, what you might call the metaphysical substrate of the world: 'the ultimate stuff of the universe'. We are a consciousness that emerged from an improbably complex — in fact, as far as we know, the most complex — organisation of matter in the universe. 'The brain secretes thought like the liver secretes bile', as French physiologist Pierre Cabanis said more than two hundred years ago, and scientists actually still think this way today. This view is one that does justice to your correct conclusion that what we are is something fundamentally different from what we intuitively think we are, but is also in line with what just about all scientists think presently.

Hugo: Let me start by saying, and this may surprise you, that I largely agree with your analysis. It is true that consciousness should be seen as something in the service of the body, as a biological phenomenon. And indeed, the analysis of digestion is revealing. But we have already debunked the idea that we are mere consciousness through the observation that our being is strongly intertwined with the will. And besides, materialism — because that is the philosophical doctrine that people like Harris adhere to — raises many questions and is not at all as unambiguous as people think.

Adam: Philosophical doctrine? I think you're already getting it wrong here, Hugo. The strength of materialism is precisely that it is not a philosophy, but the fruit of modern science. It developed through scientists like Newton, Dalton, Rutherford, and eventually culminated in a clear, logical, and uncontroversial *Weltanschauung*, namely that the world is essentially material, physical in nature. Not obtained through philosophical speculation or dogmatism, but the work of open minds who consistently and without prejudice observed the world using the scientific method as a guide.

Hugo: This is only partially true. First of all, it is important to realise that this materialistic worldview is not at all new, is not the fruit of modern science per se. It dates back as early as the ancient Greeks and was at that time known as atomism.

Adam: You mean the philosophers Leucippus and Democritus? So, science is more than a few hundred years old, is that what you want to say?

Hugo: My main point is that it was not the practice of science that led to early materialism. Leucippus and Democritus were natural philosophers, not scientists! And to understand how they arrived at their atomic theory, we have to go back to an even earlier philosopher, Parmenides of Elea. He, as one of the first so-called rationalists, formulated necessary characteristics of 'being', of that which genuinely exists. True being, he argued, does not come into being, does not change. 'That which Is, is ungenerated and deathless, whole and uniform, and still and perfect'. The Indian philosopher Shankara, incidentally, argued the same thing: no object can truly exist if this existence is only temporary. Furthermore, Parmenides argued that being knows neither multiplicity nor diversity, it is one and indivisible. That which 'is' has always existed and will always exist: a single, homogeneous entity. Now, atomic theory can be seen as an attempt to identify this true being in the external world. At first glance, this seems impossible — if anything is characterised by multiplicity, variety, and change, it is the world of our experiences, isn't it?

Adam: True. Everything is in change, nothing is constant. Which inspired another philosopher, Heraclitus, to see in that change the true being.

Hugo: But, by contrast, what the atomists did was seek the one and immutable within this changeable world. Is there anything immutable to be found there? The atomists argued that mutability is only appearance and that the truly existing consists of eternal, indivisible, unchanging atoms. These atoms move in space, collide with each other, and form clusters. All mutability in the world is based on these movements of atoms, but the atoms themselves, i.e. the really existing, thus fulfil, according to the atomists, the requirements that Parmenides placed on being: eternity and immutability. By assuming the existence of these atoms — assuming because of course they were not observed — the atomists sought to establish the existence of an external world in time and space compatible with Parmenides's requirements for being.

Adam: That's an interesting history, I didn't know it. So, the roots of modern materialism lie deeper. But science in the new age also arrived at materialism via a completely different route. So multiple roads led to Rome. An indication that something is right after all, seems to be the logical conclusion to me.

Hugo: It remains to be seen whether that is another route. According to Schopenhauer, we should not start with Newton, as you suggested, for the origins of modern materialism, but with the philosopher Descartes, who lived from 1596 to 1650. With Descartes,

as Schopenhauer convincingly argued, Western philosophy became
distinctly aware of the problem of the real and the ideal. That is,
the question of what in our knowledge exists objectively, that is,
independently of our experience, and what is subjective, i.e., that
what exists only for us as experience. What prompted this awareness
is Descartes's realisation that the world we perceive is our subjective
interpretation of reality. The world I perceive exists in my mind and
is essentially of the same nature as my dreams.[18]

Adam: That sounds very modern. Contemporary brain scientists
and philosophers would agree.

Hugo: Absolutely. But Descartes then argued that our own consciousness is the only thing we know with certainty, and the existence
of a world outside ourselves does not have that certainty. That is the
origin of the famous *cogito ergo sum*: I think therefore I exist. Incidentally, his argument that a world outside ourselves in fact does exist, is
curious: an omnipotent, benevolent God would not betray us, so we
must assume that there is a world outside ourselves.

Adam: So much for similarities with modern science!

Hugo: But what is important for our story is the earlier point,
that Descartes here, clearly and entirely in line with modern understanding, makes the distinction between the world of our experiences, the ideal, and the world outside our consciousness, the real.
For Schopenhauer, Descartes introduced with this the greatest philosophical theme of modern times. As he begins his main work *The
World as Will and Representation*:

'The world is my representation': this is a truth valid with reference
to every living and knowing being, although man alone can bring
it into reflective, abstract consciousness. If he really does so, philosophical discernment has dawned on him.[19]

Since Descartes, we realise that the world we perceive is not THE
world; an insight of fundamental importance. Try to realise this yourself, Adam. What you see, the world that seems so familiar to you and
that you consider the most normal thing, is a mental representation.
The image of this table, of the clouds, of me; it is not the world, it

is a construct of the brain. An insight whose importance cannot be overstated because it calls into question one of the most basic principles of our existence. We assume that we 'see' the world — that by opening our eyes we perceive the world outside us. But that is an illusion. Which is, again, an insight that cannot be obtained through these words, through knowledge alone, but only through contemplation and reflection.

Adam: And on the understanding that this world is representation, in other words is ideal, follows the question of what the actual, the real world is.

Hugo: Exactly. The question that indeed logically follows from this, is what the nature of the real world then is; in other words, the metaphysical substrate, that which exists in itself, independent of human perception. Or, as the philosopher Kant called it, the *Ding an sich*, the thing-in-itself. In the search for the answer to this question, for Schopenhauer another important step towards materialism was taken in the seventeenth century by the philosopher John Locke. According to Locke, objects have primary qualities and secondary qualities. Primary qualities are things that exist independently of an observer, such as solidity, extension, motion, number, and shape: things that can be described mathematically. In Kant's words, these qualities belong to the thing-in-itself. Secondary qualities belong only to perception, are thus subjective and exist purely in the observer's consciousness. These are things like colour, taste, smell, and sound. Remove the observer, and they're gone! The similarities with Democritus' theory inspired Schopenhauer to call Locke a reviver of the philosophy of the Greek philosopher. The renewed materialist conception of the world was further refined by philosophers and scientific discoveries during the 18th and 19th centuries.

Adam: Okay, I see your point. But whether we call them scientists or philosophers, the fact is that people arrived at materialism twice, in modern as well as in Greek times. And from what I understand, Indian culture also had its materialists. Again, for me, an indication of the validity of this doctrine.

Hugo: By the way, you know that nowadays people don't talk about atomism or materialism, but physicalism?

Adam: What's in a name? Ultimately, it is the doctrine that reduces reality, including our consciousness and other processes in the human brain, to physical entities that can be described by science.

Hugo: But that name change has a deeper background, Adam. Let's go back to the Greek materialists, and their motivation for the search for the smallest, indivisible particle. We saw that its existence is a necessity to conform to Parmenides's description of being, and thus to assume an objectively existing world. And science, whether unwittingly or not, spurred on by Parmenides's arguments, has spent a lot of time and energy over the past few hundred years trying to find that smallest, indivisible particle. But that search has not been successful. At least not so far. The chemical concept of the atom was given concrete form by John Dalton around 1800. Elements, he argued, consist of extremely small particles, atoms. In chemical reactions, atoms are combined, separated, and rearranged again. These atoms are indivisible, neither created nor destroyed. But this model had to be shaken up, as New Zealand physicist Ernest Rutherford showed in the early 20th century. Atoms, in turn, are made up of smaller particles, namely electrons, protons and neutrons. But in turn, these particles — more specifically, protons and neutrons — were found not to have the properties of indivisibility and indestructibility after being shot to pieces by particle accelerators. The term 'elementary particles' was then coined to name the indivisible particle. According to the current state of quantum physics, particles such as neutrinos, electrons and quarks are elementary particles, but who is to say that these will not themselves be found to be divisible?

Adam: The search for the smallest particle has proved more difficult than perhaps naive philosophers and scientists initially thought. But this is not an argument for assuming that this particle will never be found and that therefore physicalism should be rejected.

Hugo: But let's not forget that the current state of quantum physics — the subfield of physics that deals with these particles — paints a pretty confusing, or, let's be honest, bizarre picture. It is not just that previously considered indivisible particles turn out to be divisible: the idea of 'particles' as building blocks of the universe as such has come into question. Since Einstein, we have known that the mass of a particle is not immutable, not elementary to it, but is in fact a form of concentrated energy. And that mass can then also be converted into other forms of energy, such as radiation. Nuclear fission is based on this principle. The discovery of the duality between wave and particle behaviour by Louis de Broglie and Erwin Schrödinger marked the next step in the 'dematerialisation of matter', as Koestler aptly calls it. Every particle in the universe can be described not only as a particle, but also as a wave. Or rather, sometimes the particle model suffices to understand these objects, sometimes the wave model. But in neither model can matter be fully contained, fully fathomed. Time and space also proved to physicists not to be the eternal, rock-solid framework of the universe. The theory of relativity says that time and space are not separate but are in fact intertwined. And in addition, within the atom, space, time, and causality no longer have validity, are no longer applicable at that level. And then you have the complementarity principle: the idea that objects have certain complementary properties that cannot all be observed or measured at the same time. The more accurately you determine the location of an electron, the more inaccurate its velocity becomes, and vice versa. This is a theoretical uncertainty, not just caused by limitations in our measuring instruments, and is due to the dual nature of an electron as particle and wave. As Koestler describes:

> [...] if an ideal photographer with a perfect camera took a picture of the total universe at any given moment, the picture would be to some extent fuzzy, owing to the indeterminate state of its ultimate constituents. Because of this fuzziness, physicists' statements about subatomic processes can only refer to probabilities, not to certainties [...].[20]

Now I am no expert in quantum physics, far from it. But this at least shows that the classical materialist worldview has become an anachronism, superseded by the discoveries of quantum physics. Physicalism is being dismantled by physics itself. So much for your clear, uncontroversial *Weltanschauung*!

Adam: I don't know if all physicists would agree with you. Perhaps the problem is simply that reality can only be grasped by quantum physicists. The brain of the philosopher, let alone the common man, is not equipped to comprehend the world, the essence of which appears to lie at the quantum level. After centuries, the philosopher has been dethroned. Alas, Hugo, it is time to make way for the quantum physicist!

Hugo: An interesting thought. Who knows, you may be right. But don't forget, there is by no means a consensus among physicists and philosophers on how to interpret the discoveries in quantum physics or the paradoxes that have resulted from them. It is not that a new, satisfactory, coherent model or paradigm has been developed in which all these disruptive phenomena can be interpreted. Some physicists therefore argue that these phenomena call for a rethinking of the basic principles of physics.[21] But what is clear at least is that the traditional mechanistic, deterministic view that the world is populated by impenetrable primary particles moving like minute billiard balls in time and space, guided by eternal, constant laws of nature, is outdated. Now, there is much more to be discussed on this topic, also in relation to the will, which we will explore further later on. But first I want to talk about an unambiguous argument for rejecting physicalism. And that is evolution.

CHAPTER 4

On Evolution[22]

Adam: Evolution? This would surprise me greatly, Hugo. Since Darwin, evolution has generally been interpreted as a corroboration of physicalism.

Hugo: Explain.

Adam: Well, you know that before Darwin, the origin of life always had to remain a mystery, in the sense that it could not be explained in a scientific, rational way. What was the origin of living things with their apparent purposefulness and stunning complexity, characteristics that suggest an intelligent designer? Even after the scientific revolution which began in the 16th century, explanations for the origin of life largely remained beyond scientific scope and still invoked divine creation. Darwin, however, managed to complete the scientific revolution by bringing the origin of life within the domain of science, allowing science to explain and interpret the entire universe — both dead and living nature. Since Darwin, we know that the formation of organisms has a perfectly logical explanation. With the discovery that we were formed in a long but explainable gradual process, from microscopic creatures to *Homo sapiens*, the final hurdle in the physicalist explanation of the universe has been taken, making evolutionary theory the crowning glory of the scientific revolution.

Hugo: Nicely spoken, Adam, but the question is whether it is true. Let's dive a little deeper into this. First, we should be aware that the existence of organisms that are not only complex but also seem purposeful (teleological) is not only difficult to explain, but even seems to refute materialism. Physicalism, as we saw, holds that the world is ultimately made up of physical, elementary particles.

The world we perceive is composed of these particles, which also means that all the natural forces must ultimately be traceable to forces acting on these elementary particles. This reductionist view implies that there are no forces that emerge at higher levels: everything we observe in this world can ultimately be traced back to these particles and their forces. But nevertheless, we see that the world is populated by extraordinarily complex organisms. So how is it that although the world is essentially made up of particles subject to physical, causal laws of nature, it is full of extremely sophisticated, complex organisms? How can blind forces produce organisms that appear to have been built by an intelligent creator? How can the fact that all organic (living) processes and structures appear to be purposeful, namely aimed at survival and reproduction, be reconciled with the fact that everything in the world is guided by blind, physical forces of nature that can be traced back to tiny particles and their forces? This is a philosophical paradox, a discrepancy between the premises of physicalism and the wondrous organic reality. A paradox, by the way, that also needs to sink in as an insight before it is understood to its full extent. These problems surrounding complexity and teleology are as old as philosophy itself, and they formed the basis of an important critique by Aristotle of the teachings of Democritus.

Adam: And so, Darwin has an answer to that. Your complex, teleological beings were created by evolution!

Hugo: You now argue that evolution is the solution. I, on the other hand, argue that evolution is a problem.

Adam: Explain.

Hugo: Look, evolution in itself is nothing more than a description of a process. It states: complexity did not arise in a day, but in a long process of adaptation that — we now know — took billions of years. But what makes animals and plants adapt? That it happens slowly and gradually is not an explanation in itself. It at most makes the explanation a little easier.

Adam: The process is one thing, the mechanism behind it another. Is that what you mean?

Hugo: Exactly.

Adam: But we can be brief about that. Survival of the fittest!

Hugo: What do you mean by that?

Adam: Well, organisms with characteristics that make them adapted to survive, will survive and reproduce. Organisms that don't have them will die out. It's as simple as that!

Hugo: Actually, it is not that simple, although many people will indeed explain natural selection that way. But as the renowned biologist and Nobel laureate Jacques Monod said, the curious thing about the theory of natural selection is that everyone thinks they understand it.[23] What you are actually saying with your description is that organisms that are built to survive will do so, and organisms that are not will go extinct.

Adam: Exactly. The beauty of Darwin's theory lies in its simplicity.

Hugo: That organisms that are built to survive will do so, and others will not, is undoubtedly true, although it has often been rightly argued that the statement 'survival of the fittest' is a tautology since 'fitness' is defined in terms of 'survival', and thus it has no scientific content. But an even bigger problem with 'survival of the fittest' is that it does not address the most important question at all: how, then, are animals built to survive? What mechanism is behind the formation of these organisms, or more precisely, the formation of characteristics that make up the organism? Your explanation of how natural selection works describes at best the *elimination* of certain forms, not the *creation* of new ones. And therein lies the enormous challenge.

Adam: I'm not sure I quite understand what you mean.

Hugo: Then we will have to get a bit more technical. Let's describe evolution more precisely: it is essentially the accumulation over time of specific changes that together form a new or changing characteristic. Let's take the eye again as an example. We already discussed it at the beginning of our conversation: the lens, cornea, the sphincter muscles of the iris, the millions and millions of rod and cone cells... let the complexity of it sink in and ask yourself the question: what process, what force formed this organ in an evolutionary process? If everything in the universe is the work of blind forces, of elementary particles without purpose or direction, how could these incredibly ingenious features have been formed? That is the question of the mechanism behind evolution that we seek an answer to. Evolution refers to the process, but is not an explanation *of* that process. And for a physicalist, that explanation is quite a challenge.

Adam: You say Darwinists don't give an explanation, only a description?

Hugo: Often that is indeed the case. In many cases, a description of the process ('evolution') combined with a reference to 'survival of the fittest' seems to be considered sufficient as a biological explanation. But some biologists certainly go further than that.

Adam: Like Darwin himself, I should hope.

Hugo: Like Darwin himself indeed. In his *On the Origin of Species* from 1859, Darwin lists a number of phenomena that he believes underlie the occurrence of evolution by natural selection. Let me list them. First, there is a tendency of organisms to reproduce: 'a tendency of organisms to increase their numbers to the maximum'. Then there is scarcity: there are not enough resources (such as food, or water, or sunlight) for all organisms to survive. This is the second phenomenon. Together, this causes a struggle for existence, the famous 'struggle for survival'. Another important feature is that there is heritable variation among organisms that impacts fitness, that is, the potential of organisms to survive and reproduce. This together, Darwin argues, leads to an evolutionary process happening naturally. Those organisms that are better able to survive and reproduce in the struggle for existence will pass on their characteristics to the next generation. And those specimens that do not have the characteristics required to survive in their environment, will not. This will lead to an iterative process of variation and selection, resulting in an evolutionary process of adaptation.

What Darwin here attempts to explain is how random variation among organisms combined with non-random (natural) selection, after hundreds or many thousands of generations, can lead to the evolution of organisms that appear to be striving towards a particular goal, namely survival and reproduction, adapted to their environments. As Jacques Monod said, it is in this way that from a source of noise (random variation, which as we now know, primarily occurs in the form of mutations) the music of the biosphere can be created (seemingly purposeful and complex organisms).[24] It is through natural selection that the complexity and apparent purposefulness of organisms can be coupled to blind, mechanical forces. Natural selection that selects on random variation can explain life entirely mechanistically and materialistically; not as the product of an intelligent creator or a vital process, but as an 'accident', an accident, however, that has resulted in 'the greatest show on earth', in the words of the biologist Richard Dawkins. What had to remain a great mystery to scientists and materialists until Darwin, and resulted in the origin of living beings being kept out of the mechanistic worldview and seen as a creation of God, became scientifically explicable with the theory of evolution in the nineteenth century.

Adam: I see your point. The existence of life is a riddle to the physicalist, or at least illogical; at first glance incompatible with the way he looks at the world, and so it requires an explanation. But, on closer inspection, so is evolution. Why should creatures adapt to different conditions if the changes organisms undergo — most notably mutations — are blind? And why would organisms become increasingly complex in the process?

Hugo: And the theory of natural selection claims to explain these three materialistic paradoxes — organic complexity, apparent purposefulness, and an evolutionary process of adaptation — all at once. The key to solving this paradox is the fact that entities with heritable differences — differences that impact survival rates — make copies of themselves in a world where resources are scarce. Wherever this happens, a process of evolution by natural selection will occur, leading to the formation of complex organisms focused on survival and reproduction, organisms that give the appearance of being created, designed by an intelligent creator.

Adam: Interesting. Indeed, I had not understood Darwin deeply enough, nor considered the theory of natural selection at this philosophical level. Monod was right, everyone might think they understand Darwin's theory, but they might not actually do so. Anyway, now I do understand it, I believe. But then we're settled, right? Darwin explains life, and the evolutionary process that led to this life is no longer a mystery to science. Oh wait, I recognise that look...

Hugo: Not so, indeed. And why not? Because Darwin made a fundamental error. Or rather, in the apparent elegant simplicity and logic of his theory, there lies something fundamental he overlooks.

Adam: Now I'm very curious, Hugo. You're going to shoot a hole in the theory lauded by just about every scientist?

Hugo: Pay close attention, Adam, and you will see. Let's go back for a moment to Darwin's observations, which, as he stated, naturally lead to the occurrence of the evolutionary process by natural selection. One is the tendency of organisms to reproduce. Because organisms reproduce, combined with a scarcity of resources, and inheritable traits that impact fitness, evolution by natural selection occurs. Right?

Adam: Indeed.

Hugo: But what is happening here, Adam, is that Darwin assumes the existence of creatures that reproduce in his explanatory model. *Because* organisms reproduce, evolution by natural selection takes place.

Adam: And what is problematic about that?

Hugo: It is problematic because if you assume the existence of 'reproducing beings' in your explanatory model, you cannot explain these reproducing beings themselves with that same model. You cannot explain a condition for the occurrence of a process by that process itself! Reproducing organisms, combined with other conditions such as limited resources, cause evolution by natural selection. But then what caused the emergence of reproducing beings? In any case not evolution by natural selection, because you need reproducing beings for that process to take place. That assumption is tantamount to circular reasoning!

Adam: Mmm… I see your point. That is indeed a gap in his theory. And I must admit, quite a big one. But on the other hand: perhaps Darwin was aware of this, but never aspired a complete explanation by natural selection. That is, he did not have the ambition to explain all properties of organisms, including reproducing organisms. As you know yourself, Darwin was more naturalist than philosopher. He was possibly not at all interested in explaining living things in a materialistic context but wanted above all to demonstrate a mechanism for the evolutionary process of adaptation, to provide an explanation for 'descent with modification', while accepting the necessary assumption of the existence of reproducing beings.

Hugo: That is quite possible, but that is irrelevant to our discussion. Because *we* want to. We have identified the complexity and seemingly teleological properties of organisms and their evolution as a problem. And we want to know whether Darwinism can provide a solution to this. And if the answer will turn out to be negative, then we must conclude that Aristotle's objections to Democritus's theory are still relevant.

Adam: Okay, fine. But then let's look beyond Darwin. Because after him, there have been many other biologists who promoted the theory of natural selection, but in a different form. Richard Dawkins, for example, you mentioned him already.

Hugo: A valid point. And as it happens, Dawkins in particular is very important to this story. But before we discuss his interpretation of the theory of natural selection, let's describe the problem we found with Darwin in more general terms. Essentially, the theory of natural selection revolves around this: there are entities that make copies of themselves. These entities have heritable variation, and that variation affects how well those entities can survive and make copies. As a result, evolution will occur in the form of the accumulation of characteristics that make the entity stable and able to make copies of itself. In other words, an evolutionary process of adaptation.

Adam: … and the problem with reproducing organisms as these entities, is that we already have to assume their existence and thus cannot be explained by this theory.

Hugo: Exactly. But the interesting thing is that Richard Dawkins, along with George C. Williams and John Maynard Smith, argued in the 1970s that this entity is a very different one: not the individual, but DNA.[25] And in itself, this is a very elegant step that integrates modern knowledge about heredity into the theory of natural selection. The hereditary material in organisms is DNA, we know since the 1950s. In line with this, Dawkins and his followers argue that variation is therefore (primarily) caused by random mutations on that molecule. Moreover, DNA makes copies of itself, for instance in the process of reproduction. And mutations on that DNA that are beneficial to the stability and replication rate of those pieces of DNA will make the carrier survive. This iterative process of mutations, replication of DNA, and subsequent selection is what, according to these so-called Neo-Darwinists, the process of evolution by natural selection in fact entails.

Adam: Not the reproducing organism as the driver behind evolution, but the replicating DNA.

Hugo: Exactly. Now, the crucial element of this version of the theory of natural selection is that this replication can be seen as a *chemical* process. It is not organisms that reproduce — biological, complex entities whose existence needs an explanation, as we have seen — but pieces of DNA; chemical molecules that make copies of themselves.

Adam: Is that really the case? Replication of DNA in organisms involves complex biochemical processes involving, for example, specific proteins, such as DNA polymerases. Replication is a biological process, not a mere chemical process for which no explanation would be needed.

Hugo: Yes, you are right. That is indeed the case. And it's hard to imagine that this process of replication could take place purely chemically, but this must be assumed if we are to see DNA replication as a process underlying the emergence of complex, seemingly purposeful organisms. Chemical processes will either be directed at binding molecules together or repelling them. But the process of replication as a driver of evolution assumes both; molecules binding to another strand, and then the breaking up of those strands. And that iteratively. This is no doubt a weakness in Dawkins's version of the theory, but I wanted to talk about another, much bigger problem.

Adam: And that is?

Hugo: That this model, quite apart from the problems we just saw, cannot be applied to living beings. We simply cannot fit organisms — more specifically, sexually reproducing organisms — into this model. You know the title of Dawkins's famous book, right?

Adam: *The Selfish Gene.*

Hugo: Exactly. According to him, the gene is the replicating entity that drives the process of evolution by natural selection, and thus adaptations evolve for these genes. This concept, that biological traits would have evolved 'for the good of the genes', has become part of popular culture and has been very influential. But I argue that this cannot be true at all; that the idea of gene selection is a fallacy, and that Dawkins and his ilk in fact contradict their own model with this concept.

Adam: You'll have to explain that to me then.

Hugo: As I said, the model in itself is ingenious. A chemical molecule makes copies of itself. Changes (mutations) that make this molecule stronger or better able to make copies of itself, combined with competition for resources which implies that not all replicators are able to survive, will lead to better adapted molecules dominating over less well adapted molecules. This will lead to increasingly better-adapted molecules evolving with characteristics aimed at maintaining and/or replicating the molecule they are part of. Darwin's own version of the theory adapted to the modern scientific era and stripped of its imperfections. Apart from problems associated with this model regarding replication that we just discussed, this sounds promising, right? But the problems emerge when we try to figure out exactly what that entity is: what, then, is that molecule — more specifically, what piece of DNA is it for which adaptations have evolved?

Adam: The DNA of the individual organism, it seems to me.

Hugo: Why do you think so?

Adam: Well, the individual clearly functions as a unit. All adaptations and processes are unmistakably aimed at preserving the individual.

Hugo: But the DNA of the individual is not the 'unit of selection', that is, the entity for which adaptations evolved. The individual cannot be this entity, as Dawkins himself concludes. And we can see this by going back to the version of the theory of natural selection as explained by Dawkins, Williams, and Maynard Smith: because there is a replicator that makes copies of itself upon which mutations arise et cetera, there can be a process of evolution by natural selection. Characteristics created by this process — adaptations — will therefore by definition...

Adam: … be directed at preserving that replicator.

Hugo: Exactly! If we assume that adaptations in organisms have evolved to maintain a replicator — and that's what the theory states — then we should be able to identify that replicator, right? Then we should also be able to point to that replicator. But the organism's DNA cannot be this replicator, because adaptations are not aimed at preserving the organism's DNA at all. More specifically — we see in *sexually* reproducing organisms that reproduction leads to the creation of *new* strands of DNA. This is because an organism is the result of mixing the DNA of two individuals. So sexual reproduction cannot have evolved as an adaptation for the preservation of the organism's DNA, because sexual reproduction is by no means aimed at preserving it. Indeed, the DNA of a sexually reproducing organism is unique: it has never existed before and will highly likely never appear hereafter. Thus, we cannot assume that this was the molecule for which adaptations evolved, and this is because sexual reproduction could not possibly have evolved for this molecule. And these are not just my words. Dawkins and Williams drew these conclusions themselves.

Adam: Then what is the replicator, if not the DNA of the organism?

Hugo: That is exactly what Dawkins and Williams also asked themselves. And the method they applied to find this out is the process of elimination. The question they asked is: at what level does DNA behave as a replicator and can subsequently be designated as the unit for which adaptations evolved? Surely the minimal characteristic of that unit is that it is not destroyed and is kept intact in biological processes. So, Dawkins and Williams search for that specific level that remains intact through the generations. The DNA belonging to the individual does not, as we have seen. This is the product of breaking up and mixing pieces of DNA during sexual reproduction. The same applies to individual chromosomes. These too get mixed up in the process of sexual reproduction — during meiosis to be precise, the division process that produces reproductive cells. The only pieces of DNA that remain intact as a unit during sexual reproduction are the genes. Genes, as you know, are the functional units of genetic material and contain the code for proteins. These are not themselves destroyed during sexual reproduction but form the building blocks that are combined into new strands of DNA. Dawkins and Williams then conclude that the gene must be the unit of selection!

Adam: So this is the background for the concept of adaptations being for the good of the gene. Interesting. Still, I must say it sounds logical. What is wrong with it, then?

Hugo: What's wrong with it, is that it cannot be the case. To be more precise, by choosing the gene, Dawkins and Williams contradict their own model. This may be hard to understand, so follow along closely. Let's look again at the theory of natural selection: adaptations evolve for the preservation (that is, stability and/or the capacity to make copies of itself) of the replicator. And again, it is *only because* the replicator makes copies of itself, that adaptations can evolve. Replication is the sine qua non for the evolutionary process of adaptation.

Adam: Just to be sure, explain that to me again. I keep finding it difficult to understand.

Hugo: It is difficult to understand, but because evolutionary theory plays such a crucial role for materialism and philosophy in general, it is very important to get to the bottom of this. The evolutionary process of adaptation is basically the accumulation of specific changes, namely changes that lead to an organism capable of surviving and reproducing in its environment. A central dogma of modern biology is that mutations, the major source of changes in hereditary information, are random: not directed towards a specific goal, such as the interest of the organism. This is because in that case we would have to assume some kind of purposeful, vital principle at work in nature, and that goes against the tenets of physicalism. Now, the chances of a mutation being good for the carrier of the DNA — in the sense that it contributes to the carrier's ability to survive and reproduce — are many times smaller than the chances of a mutation being harmful to the organism.

Adam: I agree. A random mutation is usually harmful. The chance that a mutation is harmful is far greater than the chance it will be beneficial. That's why radiation, which causes random mutations, is so damaging.

Hugo: Yet in evolution we see the formation of adaptations that are highly complex and specific; we witness the accumulation of specific, 'advantageous' mutations, in other words. This can only be explained by the fact that the replicator makes multiple copies of itself. Let's take a simple example. As a thought experiment, let us say that the probability of a mutation turning out badly is ninety per cent; ten per cent of mutations turn out well. If the replicator makes one copy of itself in its time of existence, what happens when mutations occur?

Adam: Then that replicator will quickly become extinct.

Hugo: Without a doubt. That's simply a matter of probability. But if this replicator makes ten or more copies, then there is a good chance that there is a 'good' mutation among them. And then the replicator with this mutation will survive because it is better able to survive or replicate than the other replicators. The others will die out either because of a 'bad' mutation, or because they are competed away by the replicator with the good mutation. So, chances are considerable that the net effect after one generation is the accumulation of a good mutation.

Adam: Because the carrier of exactly that mutation survives, and the others have disappeared.

Hugo: Indeed. And if this process is iterative, we can expect the accumulation of good mutations, leading to the evolution of more and more complex traits, provided they are aimed at the conservation and replication of the replicator.

Adam: Yes, I get it now. Replication can create order from a source of chaos (random, mostly damaging mutations). More precisely, it can lead to the accumulation of specific mutations leading to the formation of highly complex, seemingly purposeful traits.

Hugo: But note: these changes can therefore *only* happen on the replicator. Because the replicator makes copies of itself, the bad mutations — the majority — can be weeded out and good mutations — which are far outnumbered in each generation — can accumulate. This implies that the process of adaptation — the accumulation of specific mutations — can only take place at the replicator level. But what we see in organisms is complexity and apparent purposefulness on the level of DNA *transcending* the gene. Randomly putting a bunch of genes together does not produce an organism. It is the *specific arrangement* of genes that produces organisms with their complex functioning and apparent purposefulness. But if we assume that the gene is the replicator that adaptations evolved for the good of, we can only explain the specific accumulations of mutations at the level of the gene — not at everything above it!

Adam: I see what you mean. Dawkins and Williams use a process of elimination to find a suitable candidate as a unit of selection. But in that process, they have lost sight of the necessary features of the unit of selection — namely that the specific accumulation of mutations can only be explained at the replicator level, not what goes on above it.

Hugo: The gene is the only level we find in sexual reproducing beings that behaves as a replicator. But that does not automatically mean that this gene is the replicator through which you can explain sexually reproducing organisms. On the contrary!

Adam: So, sex is the problem? Because in asexually reproducing organisms, you don't have this issue.

Hugo: Yes, that's right. An asexually reproducing organism could be placed within this model. Indeed, this organism is focused on the conservation and replication of the entire string of DNA. So, in this case you could see the complexity and purposefulness of the organism as being aimed at maintaining the replicator of which it is part, and the model could work. But sexual reproduction thus throws a spanner in the works. This mode of reproduction is essentially a *creative* process. It aims to create new organisms with a unique genetic makeup. But the theory of natural selection can only explain the evolution of *conservative* processes, that is, processes aimed at preserving or replicating the replicator it is a part of. Or more precisely, processes that aim to preserve the replicator that the DNA encoding the trait is a part of. And such a replicator cannot be identified. In any case, it cannot be the gene, because the DNA that codes for sex — let's say, for the sake of simplicity, the DNA that codes for relevant parts of the sexual organs, the endocrine system, and of the brain — is not located on a single gene at all.

Adam: I see your point. You have convinced me that the gene cannot be the unit of selection because it cannot explain the evolution of sex. But there are other candidates for the unit of selection, right? Species, for example.

Hugo: True, but the notion that species could be the unit of selection for which adaptations evolved — and this idea certainly has supporters within evolutionary biology — is strongly doubted by Dawkins and Williams. And in my view, this is justified. Species as replicators would imply that species make copies of themselves in high frequency. But unlike organisms, this simply does not happen with species. A species can split itself off from another species, but these are incidental cases and do not happen structurally enough to act as a mechanism for the evolution of complex traits. In addition, there is another problem. We have already identified sexual reproduction as the trait that cannot be explained by gene selection. Could species selection then explain this trait? As you know, mutations are the primary basis of new traits. Every adaptation normally starts with a mutation, so the same is true for sex. So, in the case of species selection, individuals belonging to a split-off species should share a mutation that is missing from individuals of another species; a mutation that is the first step towards the evolution of this complex trait. But how does this mutation then spread through the split-off species?

Adam: I see your point. All individuals of the latter population would have to have this mutation and none of the other population for selection to occur between those two populations. But genes can be spread by sexual reproduction, right?

Hugo: But sexual reproduction is precisely that characteristic that we want to explain by natural selection working on populations...

Adam: Haha, I see. But surely there is such a thing as horizontal gene transfer, where genes are exchanged between bacteria. Could that be the mechanism by which mutations are spread within a population?

Hugo: Indeed, that is also a mechanism by which genes can be spread among individuals. In that case, the evolution of sexual reproduction from asexual reproduction (because we know that asexual reproduction arose first in evolution) would have occurred as follows: a species split into two. A mutation arose in one species. That mutation spread through the population by horizontal gene transfer. Then the species with that mutation had an advantage in surviving and/or replicating (insofar as you can speak of that at all in species). That other species died out. And then that species split up again. Another mutation arose and spread again ... And here we must make another important point — species must not only split up regularly, but must also do so at a frequency that compensates for mutations that have a negative effect on the species, mutations that are by far the majority...

Adam: Okay, you can stop now, that is indeed becoming very unlikely!

Hugo: And there's something else to that. What is the origin of horizontal gene transfer itself? This is a complex trait consisting of complex proteins, right?

Adam: Yes.

Hugo: So then the question becomes: how did that trait evolve? As with all complex traits, we have to explain this using the theory of natural selection. In fact, the problem we experience with explaining this trait becomes identical to the problem of explaining the origin of sex: what is the replicator for which horizontal gene transfer evolved, a replicator that remains intact after this process? And then we again arrive at the species as the only possible candidate. And are faced again with the problem to explain how a mutation spreads within the population ...

Adam: For which we may invoke neither sexual reproduction nor horizontal gene transfer...

Hugo: Exactly. We can't figure it out. Sexual reproduction cannot have evolved for the species. Nor can it have evolved for the chromosome, the DNA of an individual, the gene... The replicator model, however ingenious, cannot be applied to living things. Sexual reproduction, as a creative process, is inexplicable and thus refutes this model. Living beings simply do not fit in it.

Adam: That we would have evolved for something abstract as 'the gene' is an outlandish idea anyway.

Hugo: The whole idea of the gene as something for which complex features have evolved — including consciousness — is not only bizarre but also the source of numerous other problems. First, you might ask: for which gene, then, have adaptations evolved? In reproduction, only half of the genes carry over to the next generation. An individual consists of a mix of genes, half from the father and half from the mother. And which gene ends up being part of that group of genes being passed on is a matter of chance. So which gene, then, was the unit for which adaptations evolved? One of the genes that surfaced by chance during meiosis? This alone shows the absurdity of this model. But the fact that half the genes disappear during meiosis poses even more problems for the proponents of the gene selection theory. If adaptations evolve for the sake of the gene, how can it be that half the genes are lost? This is of course a huge paradox and is known as 'the queen of evolutionary problems' about which numerous books and articles have been written.[26] Sex has supposedly evolved for the good of the gene, but half of the genes are thrown away, so to speak, in sexual reproduction! But we now know the real cause of this problem: it is — as so often — the result of an incorrect assumption, in this case that the gene would be the unit of selection. And if you make an incorrect assumption, chances are you will run into trouble somewhere. And so this is exactly what happens here.

Adam: This reminds me of the ideas of twentieth-century philosopher of science Thomas Kuhn. Kuhn argued that scientists work within a certain paradigm: a set of basic concepts that is widely shared, a theoretical framework within which one looks at the world. And science, according to Kuhn, is in fact the attempt to analyse and understand the world within this paradigm. Sometimes, however, scientists are confronted with facts that cannot be placed within this paradigm, and these manifest themselves as anomalies, persistent problems that cannot be solved. You can see these anomalies as signals that a paradigm change is required, although they are often not recognised as such. Eventually, the persistent existence of these anomalies leads to a 'paradigm shift', the overthrow of the old paradigm, and the introduction of a new paradigm that does accommodate these anomalies.[27]

Hugo: Let us not forget that Darwin's theory itself brought about such a paradigm shift — organisms were not created, but came into

being in a long process of evolution. With this, things like fossils —
which were for creationists an anomaly! — could suddenly be properly placed and explained.

Adam: And what you are now saying is that for the theory of
natural selection, sex is such an anomaly?

Hugo: The extent to which we are close to a paradigm shift
remains to be seen, but the fact is that sexual reproduction is indeed
an anomaly par excellence. The gene as a unit of selection is the unsatisfactory outcome of a quest doomed to fail. Life cannot be placed in
the replicator model of natural selection, and sexual reproduction —
which is a creative process while natural selection could only explain
conservative processes aimed at preserving a replicator that those processes are part of — is the anomaly that refutes this paradigm.

Adam: Well, at least the replicator version of the theory then. We
talked about Darwin's version of the theory of natural selection and
the replicator model: are there no other versions that can explain the
evolution of life with its complexity and apparent purposefulness?

Hugo: I don't know them. Natural selection working on the individual, the species, the gene; they all lead to incomplete models or to
models into which living beings simply cannot be placed. But let me
make an important point: Darwin made the mistake of seeing natural
selection as the dominant mechanism behind evolution, with which
life could be explained in a physicalistic way. But of course he was right
in saying that organisms evolve, and that species descend from each
other. We should be well aware that Darwinism consists of two elements that are usually mixed up. What Darwin correctly established
is the fact of evolution. It is highly plausible that humans descend
from a type of ape, and further, that all creatures are descended from
(most probably) an organism that arose some 4 billion years ago. But
what Darwin additionally introduced — and this was a true novelty
— is the mechanism behind that process. He claimed not only that
creatures are the product of an evolutionary process, but also that natural selection is the most dominant mechanism behind that process,
alongside sexual selection and 'genetic drift', which, however, plays a
much smaller role, especially in the evolution of complex traits. Now
it is true that these things are often lumped together, and evidence for

evolution is seen as evidence for natural selection. For an important part, this is due to the fact that Darwin's main opponent was creationist Christianity, for which the process of evolution was as much of an affront as the mechanism behind it. Hence evolution, which is easier to establish (think of fossils) than the mechanism behind it, has often been made the spearhead of the discussion: the existence of evolution is seen as a validation of Darwinism in general, and a refutation of Creationism.

Adam: And you argue that evolution did take place, but that natural selection cannot be seen as the dominant mechanism behind that process?

Hugo: Sexual reproduction, as we have seen, refutes natural selection and in a Popperian way. And its significance for materialism explains why we had to go into it so deeply.

Adam: Popperian?

Hugo: After Karl Popper, another important twentieth-century philosopher of science. He argued that scientific theories, in the end, cannot be proven, only refuted. To illustrate this, the proposition 'all swans are white' is regularly used. This hypothesis can never really be proven, because nobody can rule out the possibility that a black swan might turn up somewhere. But if it does turn up, the theory is disproved with certainty: by finding a black swan, we know with certainty that not all swans are white. And so it is with the theory of natural selection which basically states: complex traits are formed in an iterative process of random mutations, replication, and natural selection. And what we showed is that sexual reproduction in any case cannot have been formed in that process, because there is no replicator to identify for which sex could have evolved, refuting the theory. It is a type of refutation which, incidentally, Darwin himself suggested in *On the Origin of Species* in his well-known saying: 'If it could be demonstrated that any complex organ existed, which could not possibly have been formed by numerous, successive, slight modifications, my theory would absolutely break down.'

Adam: But surely it could be that other traits did form through natural selection?

Hugo: Here we encounter a challenge inherent in the theory. Namely, there were no witnesses present at the time when complex traits evolved. No one was there to observe these processes when they took place. And experiments to see natural selection at work — that is, mutations, replication, selection — are not easy to conduct. Thus, the claim that natural selection was the mechanism behind evolution can never be really proven, will always have to remain a hypothesis. But it is irrelevant to our discussion anyway. We have irrefutably shown that natural selection could not have caused the evolution of sexual reproduction. And sexual selection, another well-known mechanism behind evolutionary processes, cannot be behind the formation of sex either, for obvious reasons, whereas genetic drift — the random spread of genes in reproduction, which is also recognised as an evolutionary mechanism — cannot form complex organs at all, as biologists know. Which means that there must be another mechanism; a mechanism, moreover, that cannot be understood in a materialistic, physicalistic way. Natural selection, let us not forget, is the only theory that could explain complexity, apparent purposefulness, and an evolutionary processes of adaptation from blind, mechanistic forces. There must be something else, therefore, a non-mechanistic force that pushes life forward, a vital principle that makes organisms adapt to changing conditions. A force that has made some species unimaginably complex. What was it that caused the first cell to form, photosynthesis to emerge, or the first eye to develop? What drove the early hominins to walk upright? What caused the emergence of consciousness we so falsely associate ourselves with? What is that force? What is that mechanism? That question, after the refutation of the theory of natural selection, is once again completely open.

Adam: So, we have been thrown back in time a few thousand years, back to Aristotle's objections to Democritus. Are we back to square one?

Hugo: In part, yes. But on the other hand, we know more now. We have been talking about teleology, the apparent purposefulness in organisms: keeping the biochemical and biophysical processes within the cell constant, the immune system skilfully protecting the body from invaders, plants that lure insects to fertilise flowers. Life is synonymous with teleological processes. Life *is* teleology. What the origin is of this wondrous phenomenon is a profound philosophical question. But we are now also aware of evolution. We know that organisms exhibiting this mysterious behaviour are formed in a process of billions of years; a process caused by selective changes in the organism. I say selective changes because the hypothesis that, in line with the physicalist paradigm, the changes — mutations — are random, but the selection selective, turns out not to be true. So, it must be the changes themselves — at the level of DNA, but perhaps also at other biochemical levels — that are selective, teleological in other words. This broadens the question: what is the force or mechanism behind the teleological processes in organisms that sustain life *and* cause species to emerge and adapt over time?

Adam: With evolution, we have in fact extended the teleological argument against physicalism.

Hugo: Exactly. As I alluded to earlier, evolution is not the solution to the challenges facing materialism but in fact a new problem. But apart from that, the conclusion that we must draw is that we cannot simply step over life to seek the essence of the world in the inorganic. The purposefulness that reveals itself in life cannot be reduced to mechanical, physical forces and requires its own interpretation and explanation.

CHAPTER 5

Back to the Will

Adam: Good. You have, to my surprise, shown that evolution, post-Darwin, in fact challenges physicalism. But the goal we set ourselves was to figure out what *we* are. Have we got any further with that?

Hugo: You are right, Adam. In our quest, we led ourselves to dwell on materialism, to determine whether we can understand the nature of the world and ourselves through this doctrine. And this is a fundamentally different approach: the materialist seeks to understand himself through an analysis of the world outside us. But, as Schopenhauer rightly argued, we should not try to understand man from the world, but the world from man![28] So let us continue the search through introspection and pick up where we left off.

Adam: We had concluded that what we are is closely related to the will.

Hugo: Many actions, as we saw, take place automatically. There is no conscious 'I' involved in most expressions of the will. At the same time, although most of our actions take place involuntarily and the role of the self in that willing is much more limited than we think, we nevertheless feel very strongly that these actions are willed, and we do not experience any of our actions as a surprise. We clearly experience that these actions come from our will, and in line with this, we also feel fully responsible for them. We have also seen that the difference between conscious and unconscious processes is not sharply defined. Unconscious processes can sometimes be made conscious, but even if they are not, they feel — barring reflexes such as sneezing and hiccups — like our own.

Adam: This had made us realise, in line with Schopenhauer, that our very being should not be associated with knowing or thinking consciousness.

Hugo: Right. We have refuted the intuitive image of ourselves as autonomous, knowing and thinking directors of our bodies; egos who make rational decisions and then set the body in motion to pursue worthwhile goals. The main argument against that image is what introspection teaches us, namely that most actions are not at all preceded by conscious decisions. The alleged self is not there at all. But when we then dug a little deeper and tried to get beyond the intuitive and metaphorical descriptions of driver and master of the body, we came to the baffling conclusion that we do not know at all who or what we are, and we were not even aware of it! While most Western philosophers have been mainly concerned with understanding the world outside us, many were unwittingly stepping over a much greater mystery: that which we ourselves are.

Adam: A baffling insight indeed. We live our lives without realising that we have no knowledge of what we actually are. Come to think of it, this insight is actually inherent in Eastern religions. I mean, if the purpose of life is to discover our true nature, which can be considered an essential message of these religions, it means that we are apparently naturally unaware of this true nature. Yet, to realise it like this is very wondrous and disconcerting at the same time.

Hugo: And that sees itself as a thinking and knowing entity! Do you see the irony?

Adam: In any case, I no longer see myself as such. For one thing, I am convinced that what we are transcends the individual. Assuming that the individual is our true being, we ran into philosophical problems and paradoxes, such as the fact that our existence is associated with such an insanely great coincidence, and that our will steers us in directions that are incompatible with the interest of the individual. In addition, I see that what we are is strongly associated with the will. And instead of the will being associated with consciousness, it is autonomous, and primary to knowing and our awareness of it.

Hugo: That's indeed what our discussion led us to conclude.

Adam: But a question about that. You say that we are not the I, the thinking, knowing individual, but that what we are is much deeper, transcending the individual. But at the same time, there is such a thing as the individual self, right? It's not that you deny its existence, but you argue that our true nature is not contained in that individual being?

Hugo: Indeed.

Adam: But my question is, what then is this 'I', this self? What is this in an ontological sense?

Hugo: That's a very good question. You are right to say that although our identity is not contained in individual consciousness, it does exist and therefore needs to be interpreted and explained. Now, the self, the individual consciousness, the entity that we so often confuse with our true nature or at least largely associate with it, must be seen as the necessary correlate, an essential element of the representation. A representation, as Schopenhauer rightly argued, consists by definition of two elements: an object — be it an image in time and space, a sound, or a sensation — and a subject: the observer of that object. Mind you, the existence of these two elements is implicit to the representation. There simply cannot be a representation without the existence of these two elements: the perceiver, and that which is perceived. And that necessary observer, that inseparable part of the representation, that is the self: the ego that we so often confuse with our true being. So you should not think of the representation as something that exists for the subject, the self. No, this self is simply an elementary part of that representation, the representation that exists for something else, something greater.

Adam: That's an interesting thought, Hugo. Could you say: the I (ego) is not that which sees, but what we are sees through the self?

Hugo: That's exactly it. Again, the representation serves something else, something behind object and subject, as it were, both part of the representation. Indeed, the representation, and thus the self, serves that which we essentially are.

Adam: The will.

Hugo: Well, let us continue to stick to that hypothesis for now. By the way, there are more types of objects beyond visual ones, let's not forget. For instance, there are sounds and smells. Touch, by which we become aware of the body and things that it comes in contact with.

Adam: And in some cases, these sensations are accompanied by emotions or pain. How should this be interpreted?

Hugo: A good point. In my view, pain should be seen as a representation that gives a signal of an undesirable situation in the body. Because of the pain that heat causes, I become aware of this dangerous situation and pull my hand out of the fire. The pain on my foot makes me aware of a thorn I have stepped in. Incidentally, like any mechanism, this can also be manipulated. Local anaesthetics allow my hand to be cut open without me feeling a thing.

Adam: But the question then is: *what* is in pain? The 'I'? Adam, Hugo? Or the will?

Hugo: In my view, it is the will that suffers pain through the I. Just as it is in this way that the will knows joy, lust, and sorrow. Again, the subject, the bearer, is a necessary element of the emotion. The self serves, through representations (be they images, sounds or emotions), our true being, that which we are. And now an important point: our being is not of a plural nature, but single, eternal, and unchanging. Individual consciousness, or the individual ego, relates to our true being in a similar manner as individual subjective experiences of a person, which are frequently interrupted by sleep, relate to individual consciousness. Just as sleep does not create a break in individual consciousness (the self of my consciousness is no different from yesterday's), so multiple 'individual consciousnesses' do not signify a break, a separation for what we really are. There is one being. My eyes, your eyes, the eyes of any animal, however insignificant, do not belong to the individual, but are the eyes of our true being; they are its instrument, as it were. And, Adam, here also lies the problem of knowledge of ourselves. Indeed, the purpose of our experiences, of individual consciousness, is not to know ourselves, but to make us aware of the world around us and our own bodies, for the purpose of satisfying biological needs, such as finding a mate for reproduction, escaping danger, and searching for food. So this consciousness and human knowledge is not at all designed to know ourselves. Our real being is, as it were, located behind our heads: no matter how far we turn it, we never get to see it. However, the solution to the problem of knowing ourselves, that for which the representation exists, lies in the fact that with consciousness, with the existence of representations, we become aware not only of the outside world but also of ourselves, albeit in a cumbersome, indirect way, namely through the expressions of our will. The same light that shines on the outside world also shines on a piece of our own being, normally so well hidden. And thus Schopenhauer very rightly says that we do not know ourselves a priori but only a posteriori — that is, through our will expressions. Through these inner perceptions, the thing-in-itself sheds its veil.[29] Consciousness is like a lamp that also shines a small light on our own existence in the form of the manifestations of the will, and is thus a guide to understanding what we are.

Adam: And so that is the will. We are our will? Is that the conclusion of our conversation?

Hugo: Unfortunately, for a number of reasons, it is not so straightforward. Add to that that so far we have not precisely defined what this will actually is! But let's continue to take this — we are the will — as a thought experiment and dwell on the fact that with this, a brilliant solution has been found for another intractable and great philosophical problem, namely that of the freedom of the will and the related responsibility for our actions.

Adam: So, the two — freedom and responsibility — are linked?

Hugo: Yes indeed. Because if it is fixed how we will act, if this is determined and therefore there is no such thing as free will, we are not answerable for these actions. In that case, looking at it a bit more concretely, we necessarily act on the basis of motives on the one hand, and the character we are born with on the other; things over which we have no control, which eliminates responsibility for our behaviour. And this is why free will is such an incredibly important issue. As Sam Harris writes, the issue of free will touches nearly everything we care about: morality, law, politics, religion, public policy, feelings of guilt and personal accomplishments.[30] Take the administration of justice. In Harris's worldview, people are merely biochemical puppets, and sinners and criminals no more than badly calibrated timepieces. In this worldview, therefore, there is no place for punishment based on retribution since people cannot be held morally responsible.

Adam: I see.

Hugo: Usually, two main arguments are raised against the idea of free will. The first argument is familiar and based on an observation we have also made. Most actions we perform are not initiated by thoughts at all but take place unconsciously and automatically. The self is not involved in many actions, and they are thus set in motion by something else, something outside us, it is argued. And therefore unfree. After all, free will implies at the very least that it was us who set 'our' actions in motion.

Adam: But we have invalidated this argument against free will by seeing ourselves as this will. The will — whether instigated by consciousness or not — feels like our own because we *are* this will. This will is active in both conscious and unconscious processes, but in all cases it is our will. By placing our being in the will, not in consciousness, we understand why our expressions of the will are always felt as our own, despite the fact that the thinking self is often not involved. It is simply what we are.

Hugo: Exactly. But even in those cases where conscious acts of volition trigger our actions, you cannot speak of free will, according to Harris and likeminded modern thinkers. This has to do with causality, the second argument against the freedom of the will. Causality means that effects follow lawfully from causes, and is an important principle of science.[31] Applied to our topic, it means that expressions of the will necessarily follow on thoughts (in the case of conscious acts of volition) and are therefore not free. And what causes those thoughts? They also arise, according to the same principle, necessarily due to causes (such as other thoughts, or perhaps sensory perceptions like seeing or smelling something, which then lead to certain thoughts or ideas coming to mind), and in any case, our will is not involved in this process. The causal chain 'thought-will-action' is as necessary and therefore unfree as the movement of billiard balls after a stroke with a cue. This idea of causality — that everything that happens necessarily follows on causes — is uncontroversial. Both physicalists and Schopenhauer acknowledge its existence. In the context of human action, causality means that expressions of the will indeed necessarily follow from motives. This tension between the supposed freedom and associated responsibility of our actions on the one hand, and the law of causality on the other, is at the heart of the second argument against the existence of free will. For the will to be free, either determinism must be wrong, or causality must not be operative at the level of human action. Otherwise, the will cannot be free, it is argued, and people are therefore not responsible for their actions. Which not only goes against intuition but would also have huge consequences for the idea of morality and law, as well as other aspects of life, as we have seen. However, Schopenhauer, who was more aware than anyone else of this great philosophical problem, ingeniously managed to reconcile these two principles — freedom and causality — and thus rescue us from this conundrum.

Adam: How then?

Hugo: Schopenhauer distinguishes between the freedom that exists at the level of being, and a freedom that exists at the level of the manifestation of that being.[32] And at the latter level, Schopenhauer argues, there is indeed no freedom. People respond to stimuli — what we also call motives — in a necessary, causal way. And how people respond is determined by the motive on the one hand, and the character of the human being on the other. This character is also fixed, either by birth or by experiences during life, over which the individual therefore has no control. People necessarily react as they do, so there is no freedom here.

Adam: So, the will is unfree!

Hugo: But now comes the point: the will is unfree in its manifestation, but free in its being.

Adam: Hmm…

Hugo: Listen carefully. In essence, freedom means the absence of necessity, and by that we mean: something that follows automatically on the basis of some ground. In the physical world, we call that ground causes. This stone necessarily rolls away because I kick it. This chair necessarily slides in that direction because I push against it. Things necessarily take place as a result of causes. But the will itself, that is, not its manifestations, but again the will in itself, has no cause. The will *is*, Schopenhauer argues. Its existence is not the necessary consequence of anything else. And in this sense, it is free. But its being then determines, in a necessary way, its manifestation in the sense that certain motives always lead to the same consequences. But as the will in itself, it is free. In this way, Schopenhauer found a solution to this intractable problem: although man's will expressions are unfree — that is, necessarily follow causes, in this case motives — the will in itself is free. Its being is without ground, does not follow a cause, does not depend on anything else. The will simply 'is'. The freedom of the will lies in its being, its *esse*, not in its operation, its *operari*. It is in this way that the necessity of our actions can be linked to freedom, which is in turn closely connected to the sense of responsibility we strongly feel about our actions. We are the will and this will is free, making us fully responsible for its manifestations, although the latter necessarily follow from causes. The tension between causality on the one hand, and freedom and responsibility on the other, lies precisely in seeking freedom in actions, in the manifestations of the will, and not in its being! As Schopenhauer himself says in his *Essay on the Freedom of the Will*:

> In a word: man does at all times only what he wills, and yet he does this necessarily. But this is due to the fact that he already *is* what he wills. For from that which he is, there follows of necessity everything that he, at any time, *does*. If we consider his behavior objectively, i.e., from the outside, we shall be bound to recognize that, like the behavior of every natural being, it must be subject to the law of causality in all its severity. Subjectively, however, everyone feels that he always does only what he wills. But this merely means that his activity is a pure expression of his very own being.[33]

Adam: Indeed, a brilliant solution to this philosophical problem that bears so much on ethics and has preoccupied so many philosophers. Freedom must be sought in the being of the will, not in its manifestations!

Hugo: And we subsequently get to know ourselves through these expressions of the will. Because these expressions follow from our nature. And this, besides being a stroke of genius, is also an extraordinarily original thought by Schopenhauer. For let us not forget what we observed earlier: the will has hardly been an object of contemplation in the history of philosophy compared to other aspects of our being, let alone being identified as the key to knowledge of ourselves. And this is not only true of the West; in Eastern religions, too, the will received relatively little attention. But we find the means to understanding what we are by analysing ourselves as willing entities, not as knowing beings. By focusing the knowing, this awareness, inward, on our will, we can begin to understand what we are. An important part of this is becoming aware of unconscious aspects of the will, which gives us a better, more complete picture of it. We started with that in our conversation, when we examined the role of the supposed self, the ego, with which we naturally so strongly identify ourselves. Many actions take place unconsciously, like moving the eyes or the hands, right down to essential processes like breathing. But once we make ourselves aware of these processes, we realise that these also come from our will.

Adam: The role of the self in the expressions of our will is not so much controlling the body; it is not a thinking entity that makes choices based on rational considerations. The role of the self is to give the will an image of the external world through perceptions, for example the suitability of food through colour, smell or taste; or the undesirability of a particular situation through pain. Or through thoughts. In other words, feeding the will with information; information that thus acts as a motive for the will.

Hugo: Or put in another way, the I is an essential part of this perception. See how the image we have of ourselves tilts, Adam? That is indeed what the self, which we to a large extent considered as our true being, is reduced to. As an inseparable part of the representation, a representation that serves that which does lie close to our being, the will. But by looking at the unconscious processes of our will in addition to the conscious ones, we come to know a larger part of the will, and thus of ourselves. Conscious expressions of the will are like the tip of the iceberg: beneath these lie processes that are normally unconscious but can be made conscious. And once they are, once they are shone on by the light of consciousness (and subsequently we immediately feel the familiarity with these actions), a larger part of our true being is revealed. Making ourselves conscious of the unconscious is like removing a filter that blocked us from seeing the iceberg below the surface, like a searchlight shining in the dark night and revealing our nature.

Adam: And the question then is: how big is that iceberg? What, then, is our nature in the end?

Hugo: That's exactly the task before us, to investigate that. Or put another way: which filters need to be removed to fully reveal the iceberg? Because becoming conscious of all our expressions of our will is not sufficient to see the will as a whole. To start with, it is important to realise that what we know through introspection is always still the individual expressions of the will — not the will itself. It is the will that expresses itself in time as a result of some cause, a motive.

Adam: The difference between *esse* and *operari* you just mentioned.

Hugo: Right. Time is like a filter. And removing that filter leads us to a more integral view of the will, and therefore of what we are.

Adam: I'm not sure I quite understand what you mean.

Hugo: As an example, analyse expressions of the will around the theme of love, lust and sex. We learn about our will here only over time, as individual expressions of the will directed at individual things. For example, desire for someone, falling in love, certain physical characteristics that arouse lust. But if we bring these expressions together, as it were, and create an integral picture of them, we see that the sum of individual expressions makes itself known as a pursuit of the preservation of the species to which we as individuals belong. Observe how a man is attracted by the shape of a woman's hips and breasts and her youth: indications of fertility. Women, on the other hand, often select men for strength and dominance: characteristics that guarantee strong offspring and a protected environment in which vulnerable, young children can grow up. Bring the individual expressions together into a whole, and then comes — hopefully — the insight that our will is focused on ensuring the survival of the species through our own survival, and by creating the strongest possible individuals through selecting the right partner for reproduction. This, by the way, is also something that should come to us as an understanding; the preservation of the species as the true object of our will is an insight that cannot so much be conveyed in words.

Adam: That everything would be geared towards the preservation of the species, that does remind me a lot of Darwin.

Hugo: But it is wrong to confuse what is biological — because you can certainly call my view that — with what is Darwinian, Adam. What I am doing is empirically identifying to what our behaviour, our will, is directed. And yes, by looking at this will from a higher perspective, by creating a holistic picture from the sum of all our will expressions, you see that the preservation of the species is the true object of our will. But this biological interpretation does not make you a Darwinist, any more than assuming evolution makes you one (as we saw, Darwinism proposes something more fundamental, namely, the provision of a materialistic explanation for life and the evolutionary process that shaped it).

Adam: Okay, fair point. But beyond that, I do have my doubts about this biological interpretation of the human will. After all, there are many types of behaviours that are not at all aimed at preserving the species. In my opinion, most people are concerned with very different things than survival, or reproduction.

Hugo: Such as?

Adam: Well, work, friends, sports, recreation. At least not exclusively with survival, or ensuring 'the survival of the species by creating the strongest possible individuals through selecting the right partner for reproduction', as you called it.

Hugo: Indeed, many types of behaviour are not directed at the survival of the species, especially in our safe, modern age where it is easy to satisfy basic needs. Humans are restless creatures and when primary needs are satisfied, boredom quickly sets in. Hence activities like sports and recreation. Still, in my view, many human activities unconsciously do certainly relate to procreation, and especially in the play around attracting, and competing for, sexual partners. Climbing the social ladder keeps many busy. Why? Often not because of the content of any position on the ladder, or because one's work is so enjoyable or valuable, or even for financial reasons alone. But

above all because power makes people attractive reproductive partners. The pursuit of success is often about hierarchical positions that
give people more opportunities in seeking and selecting a partner
for procreation. Women strive for beauty, often putting a lot of time
into looking beautiful and youthful, which is their way of being an
attractive reproductive partner. And many human activities play a
role in creating social cohesion, an important prerequisite for a safe
environment for children to grow up in. Many behaviours, in other
words, need to be viewed through a sociobiological lens, and are often
more closely related to basic sexual processes than we think or want to
admit. And the seriousness with which these activities are carried out
is, as Schopenhauer put it, entirely consistent with the importance
of the matter, namely 'nothing less than the composition of the next
generation'.[34]

Adam: But there are human activities that are certainly not aimed
at preserving the species. Look at homosexuality. Men being attracted
to other men; that surely doesn't make the species any better! Or that
people tend to eat more than is good for them, especially in the case
of sugar and fat. That's not good for the species either. Not to mention suicide! So, the will is not necessarily directed to the preservation
of the species, as you seem to suggest. And if your argument is that it
is only in the minority of cases that the will is not aimed at preserving
the species, that is irrelevant. The fact that there are will expressions
that are not directed towards the preservation of the species shows
that this direction is not inherent to the will. The will can have as its
goal the preservation of the species, certainly. And this is undoubtedly
the case in the majority of expressions. But the will can also be aimed
at harming the individual, and thus the species.

Hugo: Yes, that's right. But the question is, what is the meaning
of this? What do you think this signifies?

Adam: I think what this says is that the will, or rather, the direction of the will, is determined by the brain. The brain determines
where the will is directed, whether that is sex with an individual of
the opposite sex, which leads to offspring, or sex with a member of
the same sex, which leads to nothing at all, or destructive behaviour
such as drug use, or even suicide.

Hugo: In other words, what the will focuses on is contingent, since it is the result of brain functioning, that is, determined by the specific neurological wiring of the brain.

Adam: Exactly.

Hugo: Let's assume this is so. The question then is: how are the brains formed as they are, and lead to the will expressions that we observe? Why then, with exceptions, is the will aimed towards the preservation of the species?

Adam: That our brains evolved for the preservation of the species, I can go along with that. Most expressions of the will that we perceive are directed towards this. There is no doubt about that.

Hugo: And so, then the question becomes: evolved by what mechanism?

Adam: Yes, I understand after your treatise on Darwin that this cannot have arisen by natural selection. And that means that there must be some sort of teleological principle at work that causes the brain to adapt towards behaviours that are ultimately beneficial for the preservation of the species. And that, of course, is an assumption that turns physicalism on its head. But that does not imply that your idea that the preservation of the species is inherent in the will has to be true. The will can theoretically be directed at anything. The will operates as the brain is structured. And this also explains the anomalies you brought up earlier. Why do people eat too much fat and sugar, too many carbohydrates? Because this trait evolved at a time when, unlike now in modern society, those nutrients were scarce. Stuff yourself, the motto goes, because you don't know when the next opportunity will arise. Earlier, we discussed that modern neuroscientists see behaviour mostly as stimulus-response associations. Well, this particular association originated at a time when eating lots of carbohydrates was helpful. As for homosexuality, its possible cause is well described in the book by the neurologist Dick Swaab, *We Are Our Brains*. Homosexuality seems to have its origins in embryonic development in the womb. Our sexual orientation is established there and then. Sexual differentiation in the sex organs occurs in the first months of pregnancy, but that of the brain only afterwards. Homosexuality, according to Swaab, seems to be caused

by genetic and other early developmental factors that cause brains
to follow a divergent developmental trajectory, for instance under
the influence of hormones or chemicals. Mind you, this biological
explanation does not imply a moral condemnation. On the contrary, I would say.

Hugo: And suicide?

Adam: This, like the cause of obesity, should be seen as a stimulus-response association being misaligned. Very much so, in this
case.

Hugo: So according to you, the will is a construct of the brain,
and what the will focuses on is therefore purely the result of the specific structure of the brain. Or rather, which (of the many) stimulus-response associations are strongest ultimately determines a person's behaviour. Including connections that are based on outdated
situations, or are simply wrong. The previously discussed modern
scientific view, in other words.

Adam: Well, up to a point. That there is some sort of teleological principle operating in nature that has shaped brains to cause
behaviours that, with few exceptions, are aimed at preserving the
species, seems obvious to me. Most scientists will disagree with that,
for sure. But I still think, frankly, that the idea that the will — and
certainly free will — is an illusion is a plausible hypothesis. Neurological processes in the form of different kinds of stimulus-response
associations, and not the will, are at the root of our behaviour: it
sounds convincing.

Hugo: I think you make a mistake here by stating that the brain
would cause the will, produce that will. That is not correct. Of
course the two do have a relationship: one of the functions of the
brain in relation to our actions is precisely to generate stimuli, such
as visual representations, to which the will then responds. We just
talked about this. What is a simple cause in the case of movements
of physical objects — a stone rolls away because I kick against it
— so the representation (as motive) is the cause of actions. Analyse
yourself, and you will experience this! You think something, you see
something, you smell something; all representations, and then the
will responds to it.

Adam: So, the response in the stimulus-response association is the will.

Hugo: Exactly, and it is here where the modern scientific consensus goes wrong in my view. It is always the will that responds to stimuli, whether its actions are conscious or unconscious, as we concluded earlier. That is the whole reason why there are representations, why there is consciousness, why we see, smell, hear, think and feel things, so that the will can act on them. But what makes the story even more complex is that multiple mechanisms can be triggered by a stimulus. Images can trigger thoughts and emotions, and these then serve as inputs to the will. For example, you see a spider. This image triggers feelings of fear. And this image plus the fear produces the response of the will. The image of a beautiful woman triggers a hormonal response that makes me find that woman attractive, but it is then the will that acts on this basis. The mistake that modern science makes is that it removes the will from the chain, and sees our behaviour as the result of a complicated neurological, physical wiring in the brain. But again, it is the will that acts on the basis of motives. Those motives are not just images caused by stimuli in the form of light falling on the eyes, but also feelings caused by hormonal reactions that occur based on that image, or memories, and yes, thoughts too.

Adam: So in the case of behaviour accompanied by consciousness, the chain is not from stimulus to response, but from stimulus (e.g. light falling on the lens of the eye) to images that then cause other things, such as feelings (e.g. lust or fear), things that collectively act as motive on which the will then acts.

Hugo: Exactly. In addition, it is true that a stimulus can generate different motives, with the will responding to the strongest one. To that extent, we agree with modern theory. For example, the sight of a cigarette to someone who has just quit smoking can create a desire to start smoking again, but it can also bring to mind his or her intention to quit and the health risks of smoking, which act as motives not to pick up the cigarette. Thus, the expression of that person's will— does he or she light the cigarette or not — depends on which motive is the strongest. In part, those actions will again consist of a series of complex actions that are innate or learned and fixed in brain structures and neurological networks, thus becoming automatisms. And in addition, there are motives for actions that do not consist of representations, stimuli delivered by our senses or our bodies that do not reach our consciousness. These motives are unconscious, which means that we want something without knowing why we want it. The motive does not enter consciousness.

Together, these two — fixed automatisms and motives that are unconscious — could explain the very complex behaviour of humans but also that of animals that strikes us as so wondrous. Consider the behaviour of insects: animals with very limited consciousness, yet capable of the most complex behaviour. Take the example of parasitic wasps again: insects that paralyse their prey, drag it to their nest underground, and then with an ovipositor lay eggs in their victim allowing the larvae to feed on the (still living) host. This behaviour may be triggered initially by visual stimuli (seeing a potential host) but is driven further by automatisms and successive stimuli that do not reach consciousness, allowing this complex behaviour to be completed step by step, like following a script. Or consider the wonderful and prolonged mating behaviour of some primitive animals, such as snails, and the surprisingly complex courtship behaviour that often precedes their mating.

Adam: So sometimes behaviour — in humans at least — is caused by thoughts, conscious decisions, and sometimes by motives without thoughts, such as pain, images, or sounds. That's as far as we got. And now another category is added: sometimes the motives are unconscious, or behaviour is an automatism triggered by an earlier motive.

Hugo: Right. Coming back to homosexuality, then: what is happening here is that through an atypical connection between a visual representation and a hormonal response, a man generates a hormonal response in another man resulting in sexual feelings. But these reactions can also be irrelevant to the present, as in the case of salty or fatty foods. Reactions can also manifest themselves in the form of pain. A certain stimulus generates pain, and the will responds to this (e.g. pulling the hand away). And this can also go wrong, as in phantom pain, or pain that simply has no pathological origin. Responses in the brain to stimuli can thus produce atypical or no longer relevant motives that lead to behaviour that is detrimental to the interest of the species.

Adam: I see what you mean. But then coming back to the point about the origin of the brain: what then causes that brain to form such that that information can be stored at all, if not natural selection? What is the teleological principle that makes the brain adapt towards behaviours that are beneficial for the preservation of the species?

Hugo: What do you think, Adam?

Adam: The will?

Hugo: I think everything indeed points to that. The same will that operates in our actions is the will that shaped the brain into how it is, and how it operates. That vital force has led to the formation of organisms of stunning complexity and ingenuity. That force that also shaped the brain is the same will we recognise in ourselves. But we do not experience first-hand the creative will that drives evolution. This will does not reveal itself in our consciousness and is below the surface of the water, to use the analogy of the iceberg again. But it is nevertheless the same will that operates here. That which manifests in time in our body as our will and is made known in this way is also what drives evolution. The will that reveals itself in my consciousness is the same creative will that gave birth to life from the inanimate, the driving urge that led to the evolution of new life forms, from amoeba to man. What the philosopher Henri Bergson called the élan vital, the vital force, and the biologist and philosopher Hans Driesch the entelechy, a non-material, teleological force at work in life and evolution — that is the will.

Adam: So, the mythical creator from the monotheistic religions is actually... the same will I recognise in myself?

Hugo: Yes, the creator and driving force of evolution! In our daily consciousness fragmented to a tip of the iceberg as our individual will, but in reality, the creator of life, the driving force behind evolutionary innovations. And with this, the need for assuming a divine creator disappears. If you assume that we are, in essence, individuals who come into existence at a certain moment in time and after a while disappear again for eternity, then the creator must be something beyond ourselves.

Adam: Who, as a consequence, then also bears responsibility for our existence. This reminds me of the famous lines in John Milton's *Paradise Lost*:

> Did I request thee, Maker, from my clay
> To mould me man? Did I solicit thee
> From darkness to promote me?

Hugo: Exactly! But we are not this individual. We are the creative force behind life, a force that empirically only makes itself known in individual expressions of our will. As the Hindus say, *tat tvam asi*, 'thou art that' in Sanskrit. That's me, that's you, that's all of us. Not just the unconscious processes that can be made conscious; not just the unconscious, physiological processes that will never reach the surface of consciousness, but even the force behind the emergence of life itself: the arduous formation of the first cell and metabolism; the emergence of multicellularity; and on to vertebrates, fish, warm-bloodedness; the driving force behind the development of flying, swimming and walking, higher and higher to the insanely complex entities we are today. That is what we are! We are one with the creator.

Adam: Am I correct in saying that the barrier between us and the creator is epistemic, not ontological?

Hugo: That's nicely put. Seen from one side, life happens to us. We are thrown into existence at a seemingly random moment in time, as if from nowhere, born in a body we did not create. This is how life presents itself in experience. But on the other, much more essential side, namely the metaphysical one, we are that creator ourselves. We ourselves are at the basis of the body, our being, our everything; we are the makers of ourselves and of whole creation, although this knowledge does not present itself automatically. Life, even considered at the level of our individual being, is characterised by ignorance. You could say that in our natural state we are like travellers who are told at every junction whether to go left or right, but who never get to see the whole map. In this sense, we are like the leaf in Leopardi's beautiful poem *Imitation*:

Far from your own little bough,
Poor little frail little leaf,
Where are you going? — The wind
Has plucked me from the beech where I was born.
It rises once more, and bears me
In the air from the wood to the fields,
And from the valley up into the hills.
I am a wanderer
For ever: that is all I can say.
I go where everything goes,
I go where by nature's law
Wanders the leaf of the rose,
Wanders the leaf of the bay.[35]

Adam: A beautiful poem indeed. But on a metaphysical level, by contrast, we — you, me, human and animal — are therefore the will, Hugo? The will to live? Is this where our journey ends?

Hugo: No, our journey is not over yet.

Adam: I am getting quite confused, to be honest.

Hugo: Then, before we continue our journey, let's look back on where we came from. We began by analysing the conscious expressions of our will, with which we are so intimately connected. Using those expressions as a guide, we descended into the unconscious parts of our will. This process was like removing filters that hid the view on our true nature. From conscious processes we moved to the semi-conscious processes (processes that are in most cases unconscious but can be made conscious, like breathing, and then made voluntary), to the unconscious processes, like the heartbeat, processes in which we also recognised our will. The next filter we removed could be called the individual. The will necessarily reveals itself in the individual, the unit that is conscious, but we also recognised our will in other individuals. And the will seeks not only to preserve the species through survival and reproduction — activities that manifest themselves in consciousness — but also to adapt organisms to their environment, to evolution, in some cases resulting in increasingly complex organisms. But our will, therefore, does not reveal itself as such in our consciousness. Consciousness is limited to the individual, and consciousness of our will could be seen as a by-product of consciousness of the outside world, a function for the organism with the purpose of things like gathering food, avoiding danger, and finding a mate for reproduction. Nevertheless, it shines only on a small part of our will, the tip of the iceberg. The iceberg itself, however, transcends the individual.

Adam: After removing the various filters and delving into the unconscious, where we also recognized our will extending beyond the individual, it appeared that we had reached the conclusion that the will to create life embodies the essence of the will. But you also talked about the preservation of the species as the direction of the will. What is it, then?

Hugo: A good point. The preservation of the species is the direction we recognise in many organic processes, not least in reproduction. But what exactly is a species? Books have been written about it, yet it remains a vague concept. Furthermore, the will drives adaptations in an evolutionary process that sometimes results in the emergence of entirely new species. Therefore, 'species' is not only a vague concept but also too narrow to associate with our will. Instead, it might be more accurate to talk about the will to live.

Adam: The will to live? I don't think that's a good description, Hugo. Besides the previously discussed 'wrong' motives our brains can give, based on outdated knowledge, or brains that do not function properly resulting in not acting in the best interest of organisms (which you gave a good explanation for, by the way): people compete with each other, sometimes resulting in death. Think of war. People eat animals without any hesitation or moral qualms. Animals kill each other in the struggle for existence. Nature is red in tooth and claw, and the will sometimes seems more focused on death than on life.

Hugo: Yes, you have a point there. You shouldn't see life in the 'will to live' as life in general. Organic forms strive for life insofar as they themselves are part of it. Each individual seeks to ensure the strongest possible offspring by finding, and mating with, the right partner, sometimes competing fiercely with other individuals. And in that pursuit, other organic forms, other individuals are subdued, eaten, or killed.

Adam: So the will to live, in your definition, is an individual's aspiration to create the strongest possible offspring. And other life forms are secondary to that pursuit.

Hugo: Right, but you can also see that family connections play an important role. Individuals with the same parents strive to preserve each other and each other's offspring. The closer the blood ties, the more individuals identify with each other and strive for each other's survival. So you see that describing the direction of our will is not so easy at all.

Adam: But still, life... You talked about species as a vague concept, but I can say the same about life. To use the title of Erwin Schrödinger's book: *What Is Life?*[36] What *is* life, anyway?

Hugo: The question of what life is can be compared to the question of what we are, in the sense that it seems like a simple question but is in fact very difficult to answer. It's very good, then, that you ask this question. Let's make an attempt. First of all, life is form; a form of matter, to be precise. The essence of life is always in the form, never in the matter, since that matter is never permanent, but always in flux. In line with this, the Indian monk and philosopher Swami Vivekananda aptly called living beings 'little whirlpools of matter'. This is true both within the species — individuals of a given species, as well as offspring, correspond in form, but never in matter — but also within the individual itself. As you know, most of the matter that makes up a human being is said to be replaced at least several times during a lifetime. But in addition to matter, the form is not constant either. Sexual reproduction seeks to create individuals that are unique in form, that is, in genetic composition.

Adam: Yes, we came across that when we discussed Darwinism.

Hugo: And also evolution is characterised by a pursuit of change, of adaptation, that is, change of form. In fact, there is nothing more specific to say about that form than that it is a form capable of survival. Again, the essence of life is not contained in a specific constellation or composition of matter, not even in a specific form, but in a form of ever-fluctuating matter that is capable of surviving as form, of withstanding the laws of entropy and other external dangers that threaten it. From gathering energy by means of food, maintaining the complex chemical composition of cells and organs, creating the strongest possible offspring through sexual reproduction, to the evolutionary adaptations that lead to necessary adaptations to changing conditions or even new species: vital processes are aimed at the survival of life where matter itself is in constant flux, but it also changes form and adapts to new conditions.

Adam: Odd, really, to analyse life so thoroughly and define it so precisely. That, too, is essentially the purpose of my striving, my life: to perpetuate the form I am part of as an individual. What an insane and surreal insight!

Hugo: Absolutely. But true, nevertheless.

Adam: Still, returning to those expressions of the will that seem to contradict this 'will to live'. Okay, expressions of will can be influenced by misguided motives, for example by outdated knowledge; brains can make mistakes, and competition frequently occurs among individuals vying for a mating partner. And organisms strive to preserve life as far as their own bloodline is concerned. But none of this explains suicide. How is killing life compatible with this will to live? If we are the will to live, how can this will destroy this same life?

Hugo: Suicide is indeed a great paradox that deserves an explanation. And this explanation lies in the fact that, as Schopenhauer argues, suicide is not a denial of the will to live. The suicidal person wants to live, but is unsatisfied, dissatisfied with the conditions an individual faces. So, suicide is not a denial of the will to live per se, but the denial of a specific life form. With suicide, life itself is not killed, but an individual![37]

Adam: In other words, suicide is not the killing of life, but of a life.

Hugo: Therein indeed lies the solution to this paradox. Now, by the way, we come to an important other point. We are the will, a will that is blind. But the will does have the capacity to gain insight into itself — in fact, that is what we are doing on this journey — and thereby change in nature, transform. We'll come back

to this later, I'm sure. But first, let us finish this part of the journey. For it is not that with the will to live, however difficult life
may be to define, we have a complete description of the will, that
we thereby see the iceberg to its full extent. As far as the will is
concerned, we are not yet there with life alone. We have remained
in the organic so far. It is now time to remove the next filter and
broaden our view to the inorganic.

CHAPTER 6

On the Will in Inanimate Nature and Eternal Justice

Adam: I am very curious to learn how you are going to incorporate the inorganic world in your story, Hugo. You yourself, when we discussed Darwinism, talked about the huge gap between the organic and the inorganic, between living and dead matter, between vital processes and blind physical forces. And one of the possible bridges between the two you have broken down yourself by refuting Darwin's theory, a theory by which life could be explained in a mechanistic, materialistic way.

Hugo: I admit, these two worlds seem incompatible; this is a view shared by many philosophers. But I argue that if we look at organic and inorganic nature through a different lens, we can see that this divide is only appearance, that these worlds have more in common than we think.

Adam: Let me guess: what they have in common is the will?

Hugo: Exactly.

Adam: I am curious how Schopenhauer made this connection.

Hugo: For this, however, we should initially not turn to Schopenhauer himself. In his work *On the Willing in Nature*, he makes an attempt but, in my view, does not manage to convincingly close the apparent yawning gap between the organic (with which I refer to living, animate nature) and the inorganic (non-living, inanimate nature). But with Arthur Koestler, whom we encountered earlier, we can make a good start. Koestler introduced a very interesting, original and, in our case, relevant way of looking at the world, or more precisely, at the hierarchical organisation that characterises both organic and inorganic nature.[38]

The units of this hierarchical organisation Koestler calls holons. Holons are units that are both part and whole: parts of a larger whole, and themselves more or less independent wholes. Holons are then composed of other holons, which are also composed of holons, and so on. Look at the organisation of living things. An organism consists of organs, organs consist of tissues, tissues consist of cells, cells consist of organelles, et cetera. And the individual, as a holon, is again part of a higher holon, namely the species. So, everything consists of sub-holons, and this hierarchical ordering is, according to Koestler, a fundamental principle of nature. Indeed, inorganic nature too is made up of these holons. Look at this stone. It is made up of molecules. These molecules themselves consist of atoms. These atoms in turn consist of electrons, protons, and neutrons. And in the case of protons and neutrons, so on towards quantum particles (which the electron already is). So, the interesting thing is that these holons have independent properties of wholes and dependent ones of parts. Koestler calls this the Janus principle, after the Roman god with the two faces. One face looks upwards, as part of the whole, and the other looks downwards, as a more or less independent whole. Holons thus have two tendencies: an integrative or self-transcending tendency, as part of a larger whole, and a self-assertive tendency, as an independent whole. Think of a biological cell. The cell is a whole, and many mechanisms in that cell are aimed at maintaining it as a quasi-independent unit. But a cell is also part of a larger whole, and so mechanisms are at work that allow the cell to function as a subordinate part of this larger whole, like tissue. And again, these hierarchies, where seemingly independent entities are part of a larger whole, and these entities are in turn composed of smaller holons, can be found everywhere: in organic nature, in inorganic nature, but also in culture. For instance, as individuals, people strive for self-preservation, but also feel part of a group, such as a tribe or a nation. Or look at organisations, the hierarchy of a company for example. A manager manages a group of people under him or her. These people can be seen as holons, in the sense that they are part of the group under the person they report to but as managers, they in turn direct other holons, in this case those reporting to them. In addition, Koestler argues that this hierarchy in holons is characterised by fixed and immutable rules, but at the same time by freedom and independence. For example, a manager is bound by the goals set for him or her, but has a certain freedom to decide on the strategy to achieve these goals. This is also how things work in nature. Koestler cites the weaving of a web by a spider as an example. This will always take place according to a certain structure: for instance, the radial threads always intersect the lateral ones at equal angles. But the spider is free to hang the web from a different number of points. Koestler argues that this balance between fixed rules and free strategy gives hierarchical organisations their strength.

Adam: Very interesting. Indeed, most organisations are hierarchical, and at many levels these holons can be identified acting partly as part of a whole, and partly as independent units. But how does this bridge the gap between the organic and the inorganic? More importantly, what does it say about the will?

Hugo: If you assume the above, the first question is: how does this hierarchical organisation with semi-autonomous holons come about? Who or what creates this organisation?

Adam: And the answer to that is?

Hugo: An unprejudiced and open-minded look will reveal that this is *inherent in nature*. Both organic and inorganic nature are characterised by an inherent striving to form these complex organisations, and this is in the form of natural forces themselves.

Adam: Explain.

Hugo: Think again of the traditional materialist idea of the universe as, metaphorically speaking, a giant billiard table on which particles, like tiny billiard balls, perform their blind, eternal dance. The dynamics of the colliding particles, it is argued, would result from certain properties of the particles, mainly inertia, indivisibility, and velocity. But this is a highly simplified and distorted view of reality, chiefly because it assumes only the self-assertive tendencies of matter, namely the tendency of matter to maintain its form (this is implied in the term indivisible; what is indivisible cannot be changed in form by anything. You could therefore call indivisibility the ultimate self-assertion). But matter, like organic nature, also has *integrative* tendencies. For instance, there is gravity. What is gravity other than the tendency of matter to form larger constellations, larger hierarchies? Think, for example, of celestial bodies and planetary systems! Big systems, hierarchies held together by gravity. Now, of course, gravity is not interpreted that way in physics...

Adam: I was just about to say.

Hugo: ... and this is why the existence of this unignorable self-transcending tendency of matter is so difficult to place. In a worldview, again, that ultimately recognises only self-assertive forces, in its purest form in the form of the indivisibility of atoms. For realise once again how strange and wonderful gravity is within this *Weltanschauung*!

Adam: But, Hugo, since when has gravity been controversial for physicists? Newton established its law back in the 17th century: every particle attracts every other particle in the universe with a force that is proportional to the product of their masses and inversely proportional to the square of the distance between their centres. As clear as day.

Hugo: The reason forces are scientifically accepted, Adam, is because, as you show, they are described in mathematical terms, cast in the language of science as you do here in the case of gravity. It describes mathematically *how* a force behaves, but not *why* this force exists, why particles exert forces on each other! This is called the problem of intrinsic natures: physics only provides information about the behaviour of physical forces and objects but does not tell us what they actually are.[39] Another things to note is that scientific descriptions of physical phenomena are in *relative* terms. Energy, for example, is the capacity to do work, to bring about change in *something else*. The units of length, time and force are (combinations of) metres, seconds and kilograms — more or less arbitrary conventions used to describe other phenomena by relating these to them. A physics equation is a description of the relationship between different physical units. So is your law of gravitation! Let alone that this formula does not describe *why* this force exists. The physical force is in essence a mysterious phenomenon that is written in the scientific language of mathematics. And note that it is not only that the actual nature of that force is not given to us by physics; it is in fact totally alien to the idea of blindly colliding particles. As Koestler wrote in his book *The Sleepwalkers*:

> The whole notion of a 'force' which acts instantly at a distance without an intermediary agent, which traverses the vastest distances in zero seconds, and pulls at immense stellar objects with ubiquitous ghost-fingers — the whole idea is so mystical and 'unscientific' [...].[40]

Contemplate this force with a fresh, unprejudiced and unbiased eye, and realise how strange it actually is within this mechanistic, deterministic worldview: a force acting without an intermediary at the greatest distance. A bizarre phenomenon, indeed almost mystical!

Adam: But you are now ignoring the fact that there are explanations for gravity that go beyond these 'ghost-fingers'. Such as Einstein's general theory of relativity, which explains gravity as a result of a distortion of the time-space continuum. Perhaps also obscure and not immediately in line with the classical materialist idea of, metaphorically speaking, the billiard table. But there is no self-transcendence, no striving to create hierarchical structures in this interpretation of gravity.

Hugo: That is not entirely true. Einstein may offer a fundamentally different explanation for gravity, but you could argue that the self-transcending direction still exists in his interpretation. But you are right, there are alternative explanations for gravity, and some of them might contradict my view, but my purpose here is not to discuss the validity of these theories. The point I want to make is that at the inorganic level, and at the organic, a movement towards hierarchical organisation reveals itself, as Koestler describes.

Adam: And so, you claim that there is a striving for those hierarchies. Talk about metaphysical concepts! Assuming a purposiveness, or teleology, in nature, and especially in the inorganic realm, is utterly unscientific.

Hugo: I only state empirically that a direction is manifesting itself, a direction that can be objectively observed, without as yet drawing metaphysical conclusions from this. And that with this, the idea of particles as once set in motion and then eternally following their course, with their inertial path only being interrupted through collisions with other particles, is incorrect. For there are also forces at play that are integrative, self-transcending. For instance, gravity is the tendency of objects with mass to form larger complexes, an attracting force that, in other words, leads to greater unity, greater organisation. Think again of a stone. This too is a hierarchical organisation, as we saw: from subatomic particles, to atoms, to molecular structures. And the attraction between objects — gravity — again leads to larger organisations, larger conglomerations of matter. As the stone falls under the influence of gravity, it also forms a larger constellation with the earth!

Adam: An interesting way of looking at it.

Hugo: And at multiple levels of inorganic nature, you find these self-transcending tendencies in the form of attraction or cohesive forces. Think of nuclear forces, which hold protons and neutrons together in the nucleus; electromagnetic forces cause electrons to orbit around the nucleus of atoms and are also the forces underlying many chemical properties of molecules. Forces, in other words, that make molecules bind together to build higher hierarchies. All integrative forces that are ignored in the classical model of colliding particles. Now surely there are theories that provide explanations for these self-transcending tendencies of inorganic nature that may be more satisfactory to the physicalist. I cannot establish the validity of these theories, and, in fact, no one knows whether they will stand the test of time. But that is not the path we are on. We left physicalism behind earlier because it proved incapable of explaining evolution, and thus life. Besides, the picture that quantum physics paints is just too muddled, too self-contradictory and, as Koestler rightly points out, suggests the need for a new paradigm. No, we are following the path of introspection. And there we encountered the will, which we then recognised in our unconscious processes, in all organic processes, and identified as the force behind evolution itself. And when we arrived at the chasm that lies between the organic and the inorganic, we saw that this gap is in fact a delusion, based on a distorted view of the physical world that can be traced back to Democritus. To reconcile Parmenides's demands for 'being' with the idea of an objectively existing world, Democritus posited the idea of indivisible particles that, once set in motion, are performing their eternal, colliding dance. But no, the unbiased eye will see not only self-assertive tendencies but also integrative movements in nature in the form of natural forces that, in line with Koestler's doctrine of holons, operate at different levels of reality. And with this, the gap between the organic and the inorganic has to a considerable extent disappeared before our opened eyes. In both the organic and inorganic worlds, we identify holons that as wholes sustain themselves through natural forces, but also function as parts, as part of a larger whole. We observe this in atoms, molecules, galaxies, cells, and organisms. As the Nobel laureate and biochemist Albert Szent-Györgyi (1893–1986) wrote:

> If elementary particles are put together to form an atomic nucleus, something new is created which can no longer be described in terms of elementary particles. The same happens over again if you surround this nucleus by electrons and build an atom, when you put atoms together to form a molecule, etc. Inanimate nature stops at the low level of organization of simple molecules. But living systems go on and combine molecules to form macromolecules, macromolecules to form organelles (such as nuclei, mitochondria, chloroplasts, ribosomes or membranes) and eventually put all these together to form the greatest wonder of creation, a cell with its astounding inner regulations. Then it goes on putting cells together to form 'higher organisms' and increasingly more complex individuals, of which you are an example. At every new step new, more complex and subtle qualities are created, and so in the end we are faced with properties which have no parallel in the inanimate world, though the basic rules remain unchanged.[41]

Adam: There is, in other words, no gap between the organic and the inorganic. We just have to look at inorganic nature in a different way to see the parallels.

Hugo: Right. And we have to recognise that with this view we solve another problem that clings to the natural sciences. Does the concept of the fine-tuned universe mean anything to you?

Adam: No?

Hugo: This notion stems from the observation that complex structures in nature can only exist within extremely narrow margins, making their existence seem unnaturally coincidental. The universe appears to be perfectly fine-tuned for life. For instance, certain properties of carbon, and the ratio of the electromagnetic force to the gravitational force for protons are exactly such that they can support the universe and life on earth. With a minute deviation from any of these values, they could not have existed. But this paradox arises because it is thought exactly the wrong way round. It is not at all accidental that they are as they are — they are so because this is the inherent striving of nature! Natural forces are *aimed* at creating complex structures: atoms, molecules, living matter, galaxies. The existence of these structures is not a coincidence, it is the essence of these forces.

Adam: Interesting. So it's once again a wrong way of looking at things that leads to this paradox.

Hugo: As with so many things! And it is not only that we have found a connection between the inorganic forces and the organic forces (which we identified as identical to our will expressions) in the form of a shared direction: through this identification we also get to know the *inner being* of these forces. The same will that operates in us operates in gravity, in fact in all forces of nature. Or rather, those forces, *they are our will*. Something that for scientists must always remain a mystery and can only be described as behaviour — the nature, the real essence of natural forces — we have identified through our method (introspection coupled with critical generalisation and extrapolation) *as our own will*.

Adam: Which solves the aforementioned problem of intrinsic natures. Gravity, the electromagnetic force... it is all the same, our will.

Hugo: Now, then, is the moment, Adam, when we can see the iceberg almost in its fullness. Our will is striving, an urge operating in processes that reach our consciousness but also remain in the unconscious. It is the same will that operates in other beings. It is the driving, creative force behind evolution. And it is the same will at work in inanimate nature, striving to create order out of chaos, bringing matter together into ever greater conglomerations of matter, be it atoms, molecules, rocks, planets, solar systems, cells, plants, or animals. This is all the work of this urge that reveals itself in our subjective experience as will, and in inorganic nature as a force of nature!

Adam: But then what exactly is the relationship between this urge and matter? Between the will and this body, between gravity and this object on which it acts, and between nuclear forces and particles? Is the relationship between the two that the first — the will — sets the second — matter — in motion? Natural forces make matter move. A stone falls as a result of gravity. Magnetically charged particles attract or repel each other as a result of magnetic forces. If I may venture a metaphor: is the relation between matter and will the same as that between a billiard ball and a billiard player hitting it with a cue? Or as juggling balls and the juggler holding them in the air?

Hugo: An interesting analogy. But here you are again reasoning from the perspective of the outdated, classical view of matter as impenetrable particles, or, as you like, as minute billiard balls. Look at my body. What is this? As we saw, this body, like everything else in nature, is characterised by hierarchical organisation. Organs, organ tissues, cells, organelles, macromolecules, et cetera. In other words, what at first glance we might think of as simply an object turns out to be an organisation of smaller parts, of holons. Intuitively, we think of matter as something massive, something impenetrable that occupies space, but we now know better. Matter turns out time and again to be a conglomeration of smaller particles. Particles, moreover, that are not constantly in one place, but in motion: molecules, atoms, electrons, everything moves in a dance guided by the forces of nature. Particles moving, attracting each other, forming an organisation as a result of... natural forces! So, the idea of the will as a billiard player and the ball as matter is false. If you look closely at the ball, you will see that it consists of small billiard balls, which are also held together by natural forces, the will. And these balls also appear to be made up of other parts, and so on.

Adam: Like matryoshkas. Russian dolls.

Hugo: Indeed. And in any case, what physicists agree on is that at some point in our quest for the smallest particle, we can no longer talk about matter in the original sense of the word. According to some quantum physicists, elementary particles, such as electrons, neutrinos, and quarks, should no longer be seen as particles at all, but as accumulations, as bundles of energy moving through the universe like waves, like ripples in a field.[42] A view, incidentally, that does not solve the problems in quantum physics discussed earlier.

Adam: Bundles of energy that are therefore not always visible to the eye.

Hugo: We indeed have to bear in mind that these 'bundles' appear to us as objects insofar as they interact with other accumulations of energy, namely photons (light), and insofar as photons subsequently reach our eye. Thus, there is no one-to-one relationship between the existence of these bundles of energy and the perception of these bundles in the form of objects. Only when these accumulations of energy interact with the accumulations of energy that we call photons, these photons move at a certain frequency and reach our eye, do they become visible. And usually this is an effective mechanism, that is, if accumulations of energy act on photons (at that specific frequency so that they are picked up by the eye), then they often act on our body as well. Thus, accumulations that have relevance to our body are often visible. In other words, what acts on visible light and what acts on our body often overlap, but not always. That relationship is not always one-to-one. Consider glass: a good example of bundles of energy acting on our bodies — colliding! — but not on photons, making glass invisible (assuming light is not distorted, the surface is clean, et cetera). Sometimes it also works the other way round and light suggests or creates the illusion of an object. Think of a photograph, or an image appearing on a screen. The light interacting with the photo or emitted from the screen suggests that there is a tree, or a person, but that is a delusion. This also makes it clear that the idea of empty space where objects are located is largely false, or incomplete to say the least. We see objects insofar as energy accumulations interact with photons, and these photons then reach our eyes — which, of course, are also accumulations of energy. But the universe is full of these energy accumulations. It is like a vast sea that we occasionally catch a glimpse of.

Adam: But there are more accumulations that act as a medium, right? The ear perceives differences in air pressure. So those are essentially pressure differences between energy bundles — which we conceive as air molecules — moving wave-like through the air. In other words, when certain energy bundles act on other energy bundles (air molecules) and these accumulations then vibrate at a certain frequency, we perceive sound.

Hugo: Exactly. And this is how bats see through echolocation. Objects are perceived when created wave-like patterns of energy accumulations (again, molecules in the air) interact with other energy accumulations — for example, an insect — and these energy accumulations then reverse and reach the bat's ears.

Adam: So differences in air pressure — and yes, I understand these are wave-like patterns of energy bundles — can be converted into sound as well as image...

Hugo: And, not to mention, these energy accumulations can be 'captured', and transferred to other energy accumulations. In the broadest sense, this is what we mean by energy conversion, and takes place at various biochemical processes. Photosynthesis, for example, where energy accumulations in the form of light are converted into new holon structures in the form of carbohydrate molecules. And biological holon structures (molecules) can also be broken down where energy is released, so-called catabolism in organisms. Nevertheless, bundles, or accumulations of energy, is not a satisfactory description of physical reality. As we touched on earlier, this term says nothing about the intrinsic nature of matter, about its inner being, any more than a mathematical description of gravity describes the inner nature of this force. Energy is defined as the ability to do work, to bring about change in something else, and thus does not describe what matter is, only what it does or can do.

Your question was how matter relates to will. Not like balls to the juggler, or the billiard ball to the cue. Time and again, matter turns out to consist of smaller parts, held together by a force of nature — that is, the will. Whenever we split matter, we do not find indivisible particles, but identify natural forces that again hold smaller particles in a hierarchical structure. For matter and force of nature, Adam, *are identical.* Matter is in essence an *active manifestation in space*, and this manifestation in the form of holon structures is the action of natural forces, natural forces that we identified as will. Whether organic or inorganic (the natural forces): will and matter are the same.

Adam: You say that the will, whether in the form of our own will expressions or in the form of forces of nature, strives for spatial manifestation? The previously identified inherent striving to form ever larger holon structures in nature is the will itself? Natural forces do not strive to form complex organisations of something else (matter) but *are* these complex holon structures. Their operation *is* these structures?

Hugo: Exactly. From the formation of atoms, molecules, planets, stars, to the emergence of life and the further evolution of species — the will is nothing more or less than an urge, a constant pursuit of manifestation in space in the form of holon structures. Mind you, with manifestation not in the meaning of 'being made visible', but indeed as a realisation, as an expression in space, independent of someone or something witnessing it.

Adam: So the will cannot be separated from matter.

Hugo: Matter — that which we see as matter — *is* will. This urge, both the expressions of our will and the forces of nature, is the urge to manifest in time and space in the form of ever larger structures. Thus, matter is not something lifeless, something static and passive, the way we been encouraged to interpret it since Democritus. On the contrary, it is an active, dynamic striving for manifestation:

> [...] What seemed firm and boundless
> Is seething matter, irresistibly
> Striving for form, struggling to be born.[43]

This active striving — that is us, that is life, that is matter, that is evolution, that is the universe. That is what we are.

Adam: We are the creator — not just of life as we concluded earlier, but of the whole universe.

Hugo: *Tat tvam asi*!

Adam: What a stunning insight. And so, does this solve the problems that physicists experience at the quantum level?

Hugo: Who knows, perhaps the idea of matter as the will to spatial manifestation is indeed the new paradigm that Koestler and some physicists see such a need for. That, combined with the understanding of the fundamental limitations around human perception that also play an important role in the problems quantum physicists struggle with. Such as in relation to what we just discussed: we perceive objects insofar as the will acts on us, possibly mediated by light ('seeing') and air ('hearing'), not to mention scientific measuring devices that often form another link between our senses and the object under investigation. The observed is thus linked to the observer through the effect that the object under investigation has on the observer, to the extent it acts on the observer, so that what is observed can never be disconnected from the observer himself; a fundamental dependency. We see this playing a role in quantum physics in the so-called measurement problem.

But again, I am not the right person to determine whether the world as will solves the problems in physics. Quantum physics is a quagmire in which even the brightest minds are bogged down. People with more appropriate and relevant backgrounds will have to try to find a way out of this. I am thus not entitled to say that quantum physics confirms the idea of the world as will, but I dare say that quantum physics does not refute it. And what we did previously establish conclusively is that with the idea of ourselves (which is firmly grounded in the introspection with which we began our conversation), the forces of nature as well as matter as will, many things fall into place, and fundamental philosophical and scientific problems are solved: our familiarity with our unconscious expressions of the will, the problem of mortality, the apparent chance associated with our existence, freedom of will and related ethical issues, evolution, the problem of the fine-tuned universe, the existence of integrative natural forces such as gravity, and the gap between the organic and the inorganic. Not to mention, the problems in finding a so-called theodicy.

Adam: Theodicy?

Hugo: If there is a God who is both good and omnipotent, how can there be suffering in the world? An explanation of this, an argument that is, in other words, a justification for the belief in a good, just, and omnipotent God, is called a theodicy. Given the suffering in the world, this is a major challenge that philosophers and theologians can only solve in a contrived manner. After all, assuming a creator would not only make him responsible for our existence, see the earlier lines by Milton, but additionally for the suffering we encounter in this world. But again, this problem is a consequence of incorrect assumptions. In this case, the assumption that man was created outside his will; that he is the product of something outside of him.

Adam: But with adopting the will as our true nature, the need for adopting an external creator falls away.

Hugo: And by seeing our existence as something that stems from our own free will, we solve the problem of suffering from evil. The world as we find it, Adam, the earth we live on and the planetary system it is located in, even the country and society we are born into, all this is our own making.

Adam: Suffering is inherent in the world, but we created this world ourselves. With it, we get what we deserve?

Hugo: In the end, we all get exactly what we deserve. Aldous Huxley argues that a third of human misery is unavoidable, inherent in life. Which we are therefore ourselves to blame for, because we have willed this life and the world we live in it is the product of our own will. Two-thirds come from malice and stupidity.[44] *Homo homini lupus*, man is wolf to (his fellow) man. As Schopenhauer wrote: The world is a hell and in it human beings are the tortured souls on the one hand, and the devils on the other.[45] We talked about stupidity earlier: the tendency of humans for oversimplification, overgeneralisation and over-abstraction, the inflexibility to step outside our frames of thought, all this combined with a haughty faith in human reason, making this world of humanity 'the kingdom of chance and error' which 'rule in it without mercy', and where 'folly and wickedness wield the scourge', as Schopenhauer observes.[46]

Adam: But with the evil that people do to each other: where is justice, Hugo? At least with God, with an all-powerful supreme being, we had the prospect of justice in the form of a heaven and hell where victim and sinner get their due. And that has now disappeared?

Hugo: On the contrary. With the will as our true nature, we find what Schopenhauer called 'eternal justice'. Because with the disappearance of individuality, the difference between you and me also disappears. We are both the same will. So there is no difference between the sinner and the saint, between the criminal and the victim. We are the will — we are thus identical in our true being.

Adam: The murderer does not kill another person, because the existence of 'another person' is an illusion. The murderer kills himself?

Hugo: Just as the thief robs himself, and the butcher butchers himself. Again, the idea of 'the other' is an illusion and rests on the erroneous assumption that we are, in essence, individuals. So, it is here, at this metaphysical level, that we find eternal justice. I mention the example of the butcher, by the way, not without reason. The fact that people in most cultures tend to treat animals badly, with as most striking example the widespread habit of killing them for consumption (and that, in our times, on a gigantic, industrial scale), rests on the fundamentally flawed assumption that they are categorically different from humans which contradicts the reality that humans and animals are the same will. 'The other' in 'we are the other' is both human and animal. However, this wrongly assumed distinction is compounded by the error discussed earlier of seeing the essence of man in his knowing, not in his willing, which makes man see himself as something fundamentally different and superior. But what distinguishes man and pig is not only small, it is trivial and inessential, since our true essence lies in our will. It is because of this ignorance that humans are capable of causing animals — and thus essentially themselves — so much suffering. Schopenhauer considered the idea

that animals have no rights and that their treatment has no moral significance an example of Western cruelty and barbarism — a very pro-
gressive idea for its time, but unfortunately still not widely accepted
today.[47]

Adam: But about that eternal justice — I wonder what comfort
it is for a victim of, say, rape to know that the rapist has in fact raped
himself. That strikes me as a theoretical construct of thought without any practical consequence. A game of words. As long as it is the
victim who suffers and not the rapist, there is no justice for me.

Hugo: Because this knowledge did not reach you as an understanding, Adam. Again, this is about understanding, not about
knowledge. If this information lingers as knowledge and does not
sink in as a realisation, as an insight, it will remain words with no
impact on how we view the world, justice and ethics. But when
you realise the truth behind the appearance, when you see that
rapist and raped are one, there comes the insight that there is
no distinction between perpetrator and victim. As Schopenhauer
writes:

> Therefore, it becomes clear to the man who has reached the
> knowledge referred to, that, since the will is the in-itself of every
> phenomenon, the misery inflicted on others and that experi-
> enced by himself, the bad and the evil, always concern the one
> and the same inner being, although the phenomena in which the
> one and the other exhibit themselves stand out as quite different
> individuals, and are separated even by wide intervals of time and
> space.[48]

Killer and victim are one and the same will. The only differences
between these two individuals exist at the level of two secondary
things, namely the circumstances in which the individual finds himself, and his character; things for which the individual is not responsible. This causes the human will to manifest itself in heinous crimes
in one person and in good deeds in another.

Adam: So if I were born in the same circumstances as a murderer
and had the same character, I would also commit murder?

Hugo: That person in different circumstances and with a different personality, that *is* you! The other person is nothing but the same will that resides in you and me, but in which the same will is expressed on the basis of different motives working in a different character. It is for this reason, then, that criticising the other is so foolish. The other, that is yourself in different circumstances. Criticising the other means criticising yourself. You *are* the other.

CHAPTER 7

On Idealism

Adam: The path we have taken by following the will is impressive, Hugo, there's no other way to put it. The image of myself as a knowing individual has disappeared. What has taken its place is the will: an urge for spatial manifestation that makes itself immediately known in my conscious will expressions, but in fact extends to all conscious and unconscious processes in this body and beyond, and both in living and inanimate nature. A fascinating, but also bizarre journey! It is through introspection '*Daß ich erkenne, was die Welt / Im Innersten zusammenhält.*'[49]

Hugo: And this reality is stranger than we could ever have imagined, isn't it? This once again refutes the image of ourselves as knowing beings. As we naturally stand, we have no idea, really no clue about what we really are, and it is only by means of this narrow, difficult path that we have been able to figure out the truth.

Adam: And it is Schopenhauer who is waiting for us at the end of the journey?

Hugo: Well, although we have undoubtedly come very close to Schopenhauer's philosophy, there are several differences between our findings and his teachings. Indeed, the largest and most important difference concerns a very essential element of his philosophy, namely his idealism. You remember earlier when we discussed how the development of modern materialism could be traced back to the ideas of Descartes, and through Locke and later thinkers and scientists took its present form? However, with Kant, and after him Schopenhauer, came a countermovement with interesting objections to this philosophical doctrine. Just as Locke took the path leading towards materialism, Kant took a fundamentally different direction with his 'transcendental idealism'. An inspiration for Kant, as is well known, was another British philosopher, David Hume, who argued — unlike the so-called rationalists — that our idea of causality, the idea that events (effects) are always preceded by other events (causes), is not a priori, but is grounded in a habit of thought based on observation. Kant disputed that: our idea of causality, as well as that of time and space, are indeed a priori. But the question Kant then asked was: how is this a priori knowledge possible? Where does this knowledge, this certainty come from if we cannot trace it back to experience? His solution was that this knowledge is possible because it belongs to the subject, which is within, not the object, which is the world outside us. Kant called this his Copernican revolution. Instead of knowledge conforming to objects, objects must conform to the forms of our knowledge, forms that thus belong to the subject, not the object. Inspired by Kant, Schopenhauer also argued that the forms of our knowing, specifically time, space, and causality, have a subjective origin. They belong to the knowing subject, not that which exists outside and independent of this knowing subject. Matter, however, can only exist in time, space, and causality, and this implies the existence of these forms, with which matter must also remain subjective, and cannot be the thing-in-itself. So according to Schopenhauer, not only Locke's secondary qualities, such as smell, colour and taste, are subjective, but also time, space and causality, and thus matter. Matter can therefore never exist independently of a subject. In other words, Locke removed those aspects of objects that are added by our senses from the thing-in-itself (i.e. smell, colour, taste et cetera). Schopen-hauer, inspired by Kant, additionally removed those aspects that he believed are added by the forms of our cognition: time, space, and causality. And since matter can only exist within those forms, i.e., not without activity of the mind, it cannot be the thing-in-itself.

Adam: So the idealists drew an even more radical conclusion from Descartes's insight? For both (modern) materialists and idealists, the external world we perceive is subjective in nature; an insight brought to philosophical awareness by Descartes and shared by contemporary scientists and philosophers. The world is representation, in Schopenhauer's words. Materialists, however, argue that there is an objectively existing world behind, or outside, this subjective world that corresponds broadly to our perception. Stripped of colours, smells, sounds and feelings, but nevertheless identical on an elementary level. The idealists, on the other hand, argue that such a world does not exist, that the world behind representation, behind subjective experience, is of a totally different nature?

Hugo: That's a good description. Incidentally, the similarities between the idealism of Schopenhauer and Indian Vedanta are striking. The idea that time, space and causality have an ideal character, and do not belong to the world *an sich*, is a main dogma of the Vedanta philosophy. According to this doctrine, the thing-in-itself, also called the Absolute, is 'caught' in our consciousness in time, space and causality, forms that do not belong to the Absolute, but to our individual consciousness. That which exists separately from the knowing subject will therefore not exist in the forms of our knowing — time, space, and causality.

Adam: But you reject this idealism. Explain.

Hugo: Let me start by saying that in discussing time, space and causality and their relation to the subject, we are now moving into much trickier territory. What we have mainly done on our journey so far is to get to know ourselves through introspection and debunk false assumptions about the nature of our existence. Then, through generalisations and extrapolations, we identified the will as that which also lies behind other phenomena — unconscious processes, evolution, physical forces and even matter itself. To some extent, our mind was in familiar territory here. But now we are treading on more difficult ground, where generalisations, extrapolations and, most importantly, introspection can no longer help us.

Adam: I will pay close attention.

Hugo: Then it's important to start with definitions, because that's where things often have gone wrong before. Idealism I want to define as the doctrine that assumes that space, time, and causality cannot be separated from the subject. In other words, without a subject — without an observer — there is no time, no space, and no causality. It is also worth noting that in philosophy, idealism is often discussed in the context of what is seen as its counterpart: materialism. Also Schopenhauer, as we saw, contested materialism mainly from the idealist point of view. We, however, have rejected materialism on other grounds and reached different conclusions. Matter is in fact will, the will to spatial manifestation in time, and a manifestation that is lawful, that is, will manifestations necessarily follow causes and motives.

Adam: The latter is critical in my opinion. If the thing-in-itself is an orderly manifestation in time and space, if, in other words, time, space and causality are an essential part of the thing-in-itself, then surely these must exist outside the subject? Then their existence cannot be dependent on the subject?

Hugo: You touch on an important point here, one that relates to what I think is a weak element in Schopenhauer's philosophy. The will is the thing-in-itself, he argues. And this thing-in-itself must be outside time, space, and causality, which are, after all, forms of the subject, not of the thing-in-itself. But 'will' has no meaning at all outside time and space. Will implies a striving: the striving for order, for organisation. And this implies change, and thus time. Will, including natural forces, without time and space is an empty concept. Time and space are inherent to the concept of will.

Adam: So, this could mean two things: either time, space and causality are indeed ideal, but then the will is not the thing-in-itself. Or the will is indeed the thing-in-itself, but then time, space and causality are real?

Hugo: That is a sharp analysis, and the right one in my view. I believe in the second and do not think that the existence of time, space and causality depends on the subject. And that they therefore exist independent of the existence of consciousness, by which I reject idealism. It must be said in this context that Schopenhauer draws a striking and surprising conclusion at the end of his main work. Knowledge, he argues, can only exist of objects cast in time and space. So, assuming that space and time do not belong to the thing-in-itself, knowledge of the thing-in-itself is actually a contradiction in terms. The thing-in-itself can therefore not be known. The will is our knowledge of the thing-in-itself that is *least* distorted by these subjective forms of our knowledge, namely only by the form of time. What the

thing-in-itself could be outside these forms of our knowledge is however fundamentally unknowable to us, thus casually undermining his
thesis that the will is the thing-in-itself![50]

Adam: Curious indeed. So basically, Schopenhauer is saying:
what the thing-in-itself is we cannot know, but it comes closest to
the will?

Hugo: Well, we don't know at all how close it comes to the will,
because we can't imagine anything outside the form of time. But we
digress, because again, I am not an idealist, I do not believe that the
existence of time, space and causality depends on the subject. I adhere
to the second option you outlined just now: the will, the striving in
time for manifestation in space, is the thing-in-itself, and these forms
are therefore inherent to it.

Adam: Does that mean to say that Kant made a mistake in his
analysis that led him to conclude that time, space, and causality have
an ideal character?

Hugo: How I would say it, is that these forms of knowledge,
the most important of which are time and space, are not forms of
knowledge that belong only to the subject: they are dimensions of the
thing-in-itself. They do not belong to the subject alone, but also to
the thing-in-itself. It is thus at this point that we distance ourselves
from Schopenhauer's philosophy.

Adam: So where did Kant, and with him Schopenhauer, go
wrong, according to you? By stating that knowledge of time, space
and causality is a priori, from which he deduced that these forms
should then have an ideal character?

Hugo: Perhaps, who knows. On the other hand, it may be that
this knowledge *is* a priori, but why should that mean that these
forms could not also belong to the external world? So perhaps
Kant's proposed link between a priori knowledge and idealism is
not justified. But I do not want to go into Kant's teaching or any
possible errors in it, because my arguments against idealism are of
an entirely different nature. Arguments that I hope will convince
everyone that it is not possible for time, space and causality to exist
only in the subject.

Adam: I am all ears.

Hugo: First of all: the role that consciousness plays, the function it has for the body is so obvious that there can be no question about its secondary nature compared to the latter. We discussed this earlier: consciousness is entirely at the service of the body. It maps the environment so that danger can be averted, food can be gathered, and mates can be found. Consciousness only makes sense, its existence can only be understood in the context of the organism it evolved for. And what is an organism? An entity located in time and space, trying to survive and reproduce in this world. Consciousness is a biological phenomenon par excellence, evolved as such, and therefore cannot be seen as otherwise than secondary to the — physical — body (to be clear: when I speak of body, I do not imply a material body, but a hierarchical organisation in time and space, in line with what we just discussed). This biological context would also explain why our knowledge of time, space and causality can be a priori, and yet belong to the world *an sich*, to return to Kant. In this case, time, space, and causality are 'hard-wired', ingrained in our mental faculties and therefore a priori, with the aim of creating in our minds a kind of copy of the world, the world *an sich* that is also characterised by these forms. Incidentally, this biological image of man — and thus of consciousness — is a relative novelty, originating with Darwin, who fundamentally changed the image of the human species with his idea of evolution (and again, with the introduction of evolution he was right, with natural selection he was wrong). Man is not a being created after God's likeness, but a biological being descended from an ape-like animal, which in turn eventually evolved from a first life form in the primordial soup billions of years ago, in a long and hard struggle for existence. The body is primary, consciousness secondary.

Adam: So, the belief in the primacy of consciousness — and thus of the subject — is actually a pre-evolutionary anthropocentric position? Because you're right, evolution undermines idealism, the doctrine that gives the subject a very prominent ontological status.

Hugo: Indeed. The *biological* function of consciousness has strong *ontological* implications. And then there is another — second — argument against idealism related to the biological nature of consciousness: the phenomenon of ancestrality, a term coined by

French philosopher Quentin Meillassoux.[51] It refers to the fact that science today can make accurate statements about events that took place before there was consciousness, and therefore before there were subjects. Indeed, before life existed at all. The creation of the universe 13.5 billion years ago, that of the earth 4.5 billion, the first forms of life 3.5 billion years ago, the first animals, humans and so on. Although there can of course be a debate about the exact timing of those events, we have to assume their actual occurrence to explain the emergence of conscious beings. Surely this means that there was a manifesting will in time and space before there was consciousness at all.

Adam: That is indeed a very strong argument in favour of the position that time and space cannot depend on the existence of the subject.

Hugo: And, interestingly, Schopenhauer says something similar in his work:

> […] the law of causality, and the consideration and the investigation of nature which follow on it, lead us necessarily to the certain assumption that each more highly organized state of matter succeeded in time a cruder state. Thus animals existed before men, fishes before land animals, plants before fishes, and the inorganic before that which is organic; consequently the original mass had to go through a long series of changes before the first eye could be opened.[52]

Adam: By which Schopenhauer acknowledges the existence of the process of evolution?

Hugo: Which, as a side note, indeed shows that evolution, regardless of the mechanism behind it, was not Darwin's discovery, and indeed, was already posited by Schopenhauer! But then he says:

> And yet the existence of this whole world remains for ever dependent on that first eye that opened, were it even that of an insect.

Adam: Which is in line with his idealism. After all, without a subject there is no object!

Hugo: So, we see that, according to Schopenhauer, on the one hand the existence of the whole world depends on the first knowing being, and how, on the other hand, the existence of this first knowing being is completely dependent on a long chain of causes and effects that preceded it. Schopenhauer regards this as an antinomy associated with the materialistic worldview.

Adam: An antinomy?

Hugo: An antinomy, a term adopted by Kant, is two propositions that follow logically from a certain worldview but contradict each other at the same time: a sort of philosophical paradox, in other words. And this contradiction results from the fact that this worldview is incorrect.

Adam: I don't quite understand what you mean.

Hugo: See, for example, Kant's famous first antinomy:

Thesis — the world (universe) has a beginning and an end in time and space

Antithesis — the world is unlimited in terms of time and space; it has no beginning and no limits in space. These propositions are both correct, yet they contradict each other. According to Kant, this is because we incorrectly view the external world as objectively existing, independent of the subject, a view he calls transcendental realism and is shared with the doctrine of materialism. So again, an antinomy is the consequence of adopting the wrong worldview.

Adam: This is in line with what you yourself regularly noted: paradoxes arise from incorrect assumptions.

Hugo: But there is a fundamental difference between Kant's antinomies and Schopenhauer's. Kant's antinomies were based on alleged internal contradictions within what he believed to be an erroneous worldview, in this case transcendental realism. But Schopenhauer is demonstrating contradictions within his own transcendental idealism!

Adam: So, within his own worldview.

Hugo: Exactly. Because mind you, according to materialism, matter does not depend on the subject at all, and so a world could perfectly well have existed before the emergence of the first subject.

Thus, for the materialist, the whole world was not at all dependent on that first eye that opened. Thus, he ascribes the thesis 'the existence of that whole world was dependent on that first eye opening' to materialism, but what Schopenhauer is unwittingly doing here with this antinomy, is undermining his own transcendental idealism. This antinomy (the existence of a long chain of changes before the first eye could open, but the dependence of this chain on the first eye that opened) relates to *his* teaching, not that of materialism. Schopenhauer's antinomy actually reveals the problem of ancestrality.

Adam: Interesting. If idealism is an anthropocentric worldview that puts too much emphasis on the knowing element of human beings, it is ironic that Schopenhauer was an idealist since he relativised this feature like no other and contrasted it with the will as the essential feature of *Homo sapiens*.

Hugo: That's absolutely correct. In this sense, his philosophy consists of two elements that are incompatible, immiscible like water and oil. On the one hand is his idealism, inspired by Kant and Plato and very similar to the teachings of the Upanishads and Vedanta that he admired. On the other hand, however, is his particularly original philosophy that posits the will as the thing-in-itself, a doctrine that represents a devaluation of the importance of the knowing element in humans. A strange mixture that leads to contradictions. How about this one, for instance? According to the idealist Schopenhauer, time, space, and causality exist within the subject. And thus, the subject itself falls outside these forms:

> [...] the subject, the knowing never the known, does not lie within those forms; on the contrary, it is always presupposed by those forms themselves, and hence neither plurality, nor its opposite, namely unity, belongs to it.[53]

Adam: Clearly an idealistic point of view.

Hugo: Certainly. Only one can question 'nor its opposite'. Schopenhauer has a point that multiplicity can only exist within the forms time and space. But anything that exists outside these forms must therefore be one and indivisible according to that same logic, despite what Schopenhauer argues here. For something that exists outside time, space, and causality is necessarily omnipresent, eternal and indivisible. You no doubt recognise this description.

Adam: 'Being' according to Parmenides and Shankara.

Hugo: Exactly. If time, space, and causality exist only within the subject and the subject itself is outside these forms, then this automatically makes the subject eternal, immutable, indivisible.

Adam: The thing-in-itself!

Hugo: Right. But Schopenhauer himself contradicts this ('to the subject neither plurality, nor its opposite, namely unity, belongs to it'), incidentally without clarifying this. And it is obvious why he is forced to do so. After all, according to his doctrine, the subject is not the thing-in-itself, but the will. But that does not make this thesis correct. 'No multiplicity' simply implies that the subject is eternal, immutable, indivisible. By exclusively placing the forms time, space, and causality within the subject, you automatically imply that the subject is the thing-in-itself, notwithstanding Schopenhauer's (poor) reasoning.

Adam: You cannot adhere to idealism without giving the subject a prominent ontological status.

Hugo: Exactly. By consequence, many followers of the Vedanta philosophy identify Brahman (the thing-in-itself) as, or at least associate it with, consciousness, often described as *sat-chit-ananda* — truth-consciousness-bliss.

However, other contradictions can be found in Schopenhauer that can be traced back to his idealism. For instance, when he discusses the role of the brain. As we saw, Schopenhauer posits the subject as a condition for the existence of the object — there are no objects without subjects (and, for that matter, no subjects without objects). Indeed, that is what idealism, for which the subject is the bearer of the world, the condition of all that is object, states. So, there is also no matter without the subject. But on the other hand, Schopenhauer argues that it is the brain that generates representations in time and space. That what exists objectively is cast by the brain into the forms of time, space, and causality, he claims.[54] But in doing so, he undermines his own narrative. What he thereby implies is that brains — consisting of matter existing in space and time — exist before the representation itself. But surely space and time would exist only in consciousness? That is after all what idealism states. So, Schopenhauer here assumes the existence of matter before the representation, i.e., before the subject. And with this, he contradicts idealism.

Adam: That is indeed a very remarkable point. A major inconsistency in his thinking, it seems to me.

Hugo: Agreed. But Schopenhauer is, of course, correct when he argues that brains stand at the basis of our consciousness (something that is thus inconsistent with his idealism). One could see this dependence of consciousness on the brain as a *third* objection to idealism, alongside the biological role of consciousness and the notion of ancestrality. How do we see? Light falls on the retina, is then converted into electrical impulses and transmitted to the brain, as we mentioned when we began our conversation. So does hearing. Consider also sleeping and waking, and how that difference can be localised to certain parts of the brain. Or take the relationship between physical interventions and altered consciousness. Look at narcotics, clearly showing that chemical processes affect our consciousness. Or consider that consciousness disappears when the brain is destroyed.

Adam: Now you're starting to sound like a materialist, Hugo!

Hugo: That is certainly not the intention, so let me clear up that misunderstanding immediately. As we concluded earlier: matter is nothing but the will itself, the will for spatial manifestation. As such, the brain is also more than a constellation or aggregation of molecules, of matter. Just as matter in general is the will to manifestation, the brain — next to all its other functions — is the will to consciousness, to awareness. It is the creative potential of the will, a creative force capable of producing this consciousness.

Adam: This statement is not really satisfactory, I must say.

Hugo: If there was an easier, simpler solution to this great philosophical problem, don't you think it would have been found long ago?

Adam: Yes, haha, that's a good one.

Hugo: It remains difficult for our minds to grasp, but then they are not designed to understand this. But at least explaining consciousness from the will is less problematic than explaining consciousness from matter; a problem that materialism faces. 'The brain secretes thought like the liver secretes bile': but the problem is precisely that consciousness is something fundamentally different from bile. It is not a chemical process we are talking about, a transition from substance A to substance B, but a transition from a substance — the brain — to something of a fundamentally different nature: consciousness. Today, we know a lot about the topography of the brain, its embryonic development and functioning, and can link these to behaviour and mental processes. But no matter how much you understand of this, for modern science brains remain molecules, matter. And the gap between this matter and consciousness remains wide. How can consciousness emerge from matter? Australian philosopher David Chalmers calls this 'the hard problem of consciousness', and this problem is still waiting to be solved. As philosopher Philip Goff says: 'Nothing is more certain than consciousness, and yet nothing is harder to incorporate into our scientific picture of the world.'[55]

Adam: But don't you face a similar problem, Hugo? Isn't the step from will to consciousness the same as the step from matter to consciousness? A bit easy to invoke the limits of knowledge. There was, according to your reasoning, apparently a time when the will 'manifested in space' without a consciousness to perceive it. Then, at some point, consciousness arises and with it, ontological novelties — images in time and space, colours, smells, feelings, sound. This too, Hugo, is ontologically of an entirely different nature than the 'spatial manifestations in space'.

Hugo: You have a point. But again, I think this is simply one of those issues that is beyond our intellectual capacities to grasp completely, however frustrating that may be. Let us also remember what consciousness is for. It evolved for the purpose of getting a view of the world through perception, images, sounds, smells, what Schopenhauer calls intuitive representations, and concepts, so-called abstract representations. But the mind is not designed to understand itself. Its cognitive potential is directed towards the external world, it is a part of the body with a distinct role and function within the whole. So there are simply limits to understanding, and this is one such limit.

But we must assume, however unsatisfactory it may be, that the will is a creative force and has the potential to create images, feelings, touch, sounds, pain, colours. Incidentally, this problem is not exclusively ours. Every monistic philosophy, every philosophical doctrine that holds that reality consists of only one reality or substance, has the challenge of making sense of the plurality of experience. This is especially the case for those philosophical systems that assume the existence of evolutionary processes, processes characterised by the emergence of novelties over time. But again, just as matter in general is the will to manifestation, brains in particular are the will to perception, to consciousness. It is the creative potential of the will, a creative force capable of producing these things. As part of the will to manifestation, we here encounter the will to see, to perceive, to consciousness, entirely within the framework of this universal will to manifestation.

Adam: I continue to find it a wondrous thing. Imagine sitting in a theatre and watching a musical performance. So first, you must realise that what you are experiencing is a subjective experience. The musician on stage is not a musician per se: it is a representation of a musician. This artist that I see exists as such in my consciousness. Again, what a wondrous, yes almost bizarre fact when you realise it! But what *actually* exists, you argue, are will manifestations, as also in the case of that musician. A will manifestation in the form of a holon, which via light — also a manifestation of the will — reaches another will manifestation, that which I experience as my body.

Hugo: That's absolutely right. But again, how difficult it is to hold on to this understanding, this insight, and not take the world I perceive as the true world!

Adam: And when I look around me, at all the other spectators watching the performance: they too have these representations, just like me. But that means that there are hundreds of parallel representations, in addition to the world of will manifestations as such. But my question then is: where are these representations? In space? Here, in my head? No, the representation is not in my head. In my head there is nothing but grey and white matter, right? Open my skull and you will find nothing but brains there.

Hugo: Well, to be precise, this is not correct. Your brain does not exist in itself. Brains only exist as representations.

Adam: Okay, fair point. The world as such consists of will manifestations in space. So instead of brain I should say: the spatial holon structure I perceive as brain. But the problem remains. *Where* are these other hundreds of representations? All those images, representations, of all these spectators?

Hugo: That's a very good question. Look at me and you know: a consciousness is associated with this individual. There is something that has an image of Adam, perceives sounds, has thoughts. Now it is impossible to place these representations — which you know exist! — in space. Not in the space you perceive — because there you find only matter — nor in space as such, the space where the will manifests itself.

Adam: Exactly.

Hugo: The first step in solving this problem is not to seek these representations in the individual. As we concluded earlier: the ego is not that which sees, but instead that which we are — the will in other words — sees through the self. Our being is not plural, but single, eternal and unchanging. It is that single will that sees, not the self, the individual. This also means that we should not place that representation in that particular place in space where the individual is. Look at me — through this body, through this holon of spatial manifestation that we perceive as the brain, an image is generated; it is an image of you, but it is not the individual, this I, that sees, but the will itself. Therefore, you should not look for that image where this individual is! Coming back to your theatre: yes, there are hundreds of representations, but those representations belong to the will, not to these individuals. There is one being, our experiences belong to this being, and therefore are not to be found at those individuals. Further, representations are not in space. And I mean absolute space, not the space of my subjective experience. Representations are in another dimension, as it were. Incidentally, just as sounds, pain, sensations in general are neither in space. We don't ask where sound is, or where pain is, do we? Yes, perhaps where the origin of pain or sound is, but the sensations themselves are not to be found in space.

Adam: That's a good point.

Hugo: By the way, this question — for whom and where does perception take place — also plays a role in the discussion around the homunculus argument.

Adam: Homunculus?

Hugo: The homunculus, derived from the Latin for 'little man,' is a philosophical concept that suggests there is an entity within the brain, something or even someone, that perceives the images transmitted through the senses.

Adam: A ludicrous theory, seen with today's knowledge.

Hugo: Certainly, totally incompatible with modern scientific ideas about how the brain works. But what is interesting is the right philosophical question that underlies this theory: what actually sees, and where does it reside? Consider again the biochemistry behind vision — light is projected onto the retina, then millions of rod and cone cells with their sophisticated structures convert the light into electrical signals that are then transported to the brain where they are ingeniously processed. That knowledge, or rather, that understanding, automatically raises the question: where does perception then take place? When and by what are these signals translated into images?

Adam: That is indeed a very legitimate question if you step over superficial notions of seeing and contemplate its underlying physiology. Who or what really sees? And where does that reside?

Hugo: And postulating an inner observer in the brain — a homunculus — does not solve this problem. Also because, as is well known, this leads to a regression problem: if there was a small something or someone in the brain looking at the images, the question can be asked how this entity then sees. Assuming an even smaller observer responsible for that entity's perceptions, you end up with an infinite regression; you are actually shifting the problem. No, answering this question — what really sees, and where does it reside — requires a fundamentally different solution and cannot be solved by placing the viewer within space and within the individual. The will, the one, undivided, beyond time and space, that is what sees, that is what perceives! To recognise that, Adam, is to discover your true nature!

Adam: Although the insight is beginning to dawn on me, it still sounds vague and difficult to understand. It is the will that perceives, and all perceptions belong to that same will?

Hugo: The will sees through my brain (that is, the complex holon structure we perceive as a brain), through your brain, et cetera. Think of the individual as the eye through which the will sees!

Adam: It remains difficult to understand it.

Hugo: Be aware that materialists also struggle with locating consciousness in space, perhaps even more so because they associate consciousness much more with the individual.[56] And idealists also face this challenge: how to deal with different consciousnesses, how to locate them, place them in space, and how to relate them to the brain. It's simply an area that our minds can't quite reach. But by positing that which sees as the will, not the individual, but the will that exists everywhere and always, the will with which the universe is, as it were, interwoven, we solve the problem, however difficult it remains to understand. That which perceives need not be localised or assumed to be in one place, like a small person in the brain. It is the thing-in-itself, the One and All, that sees.

Adam: As a sensibility that permeates the universe?

Hugo: Exactly. What brains in fact do is deliver streams of data and transform this data into an image of the world, or sound, or pain. Which the will then responds to, as we discussed earlier.

Adam: Yet the gap between these data streams and the creation of a conscious experience, a representation, remains very large. I mean, how is it possible for an image to emerge from these electrical signals?

Hugo: Again, you should not think of the brain as a constellation of molecules, of matter. Just as matter in general is the will to manifestation, brains in combination with the senses are the will to perception, to consciousness.

Adam: Yes, you said it — it is the creative potential of the will, a creative force capable of bringing forth this consciousness.

Hugo: That's how you should see the will, indeed.

Adam: I believe it is beginning to dawn on me, Hugo, but it is still very hard to grasp.

Hugo: As I warned you, we are entering a challenging, obscure territory now. But let's finish our earlier topic, namely reasons why we should reject idealism, so that we can at least close this path and not complicate matters even more. We have discussed the biological-functional argument, the problem of ancestrality, and the brain as a condition for the existence of the subject as arguments against idealism, the doctrine that assumes that time, space, and causality cannot exist without a subject. Now we can extend this last argument — brains as a condition for the existence of the subject — to other phenomena as well. Namely, we simply cannot understand reality as we perceive and experience it without assuming a reality in time and space that is not only not visible, but in many cases cannot be made visible. To name but a few: electricity, magnetism, and radioactivity. All things that no one has observed, and some, such as quantum mechanical phenomena, that are also in principle unobservable, but whose existence is undeniably a prerequisite for the existence of visible reality. Think of all the concrete technological applications based on these, such as radio, mobile phones, X-rays, you name it.

Adam: Or consider the biochemical and genetic origins of bodily processes, including diseases and abnormalities.

Hugo: Exactly. All of this shows conclusively that there is a non-visible world in time and space that forms the basis of our visible world, the world of our representations. So, in contrast with Schopenhauer's idealistic thesis 'there is no object without a subject', we must conclude: without assuming a world that has existed without a subject (ancestrality); without assuming objects that precede consciousness and thus the subject (brain) as well as those that are necessarily outside the subject (the non-visible world just discussed), there can be no objects perceived by a subject at all. And again, by objects we mean spatial will-manifestations, which we had previously identified as the thing-in-itself behind matter.

Adam: So, the will existed prior to consciousness, and it manifested itself in space just as it does now, although there was no one to perceive it?

Hugo: The fact that we cannot talk about the will without time and space and that consciousness can only be understood as functioning for a 'body' located in time and space, plus the principle of ancestrality lead me to conclude that, yes.

Adam: So then, according to you, we must assume that time and space existed before the first conscious beings appeared in evolution, right?

Hugo: Definitely.

Adam: And that the will manifested in space before there was anyone to perceive it — in the form of matter.

Hugo: Exactly.

Adam: That is extremely difficult to grasp, though, and difficult to imagine. The will manifested itself in space in the form of galaxies, planets, organisms, without anything or anyone perceiving it?

Hugo: It is not only difficult to imagine, but impossible to imagine! After all, an image, a presentation, implies things like position, distance, but equally an observer, a subject. But the latter is exactly what we want to think away. However, you cannot possibly form an image of something without implying a subject. That is an oxymoron. But it would be wrong to apply this limitation relating to the *representation* to the *thing-in-itself*. If we cannot imagine it, that does not mean that it cannot exist!

Adam: Again, a limitation of our intellect.

Hugo: Right. An unsatisfactory but insurmountable barrier. But we must nevertheless assume that this will, in the form of spatial manifestation, exists in itself. While Schopenhauer regarded the true nature of the will as unknowable since it lies outside the subjective forms of our cognition, we have come to the conclusion that the will, the thing-in-itself, is a manifestation in time and space under the principle of causality.

Adam: But now I have to think back to Parmenides's and Shankara's requirements of the true reality: that what truly exists does not arise, does not change, and does not disappear. It knows neither multiplicity nor diversity and is one and indivisible. That which is, has always existed and will always exist: a single, homogeneous entity. But something that exists in time and space and is subject to causality, does it meet these requirements?

Hugo: The will is the manifestation in space that manifests itself orderly in time. As we saw, that striving and manifestation are one. That manifestation is that will, but it is omnipresent and eternal. Do not confuse individual expressions with the striving that reveals itself in all phenomena or associate things like plurality, position, and distance with that will, things that only exist in the representation where the will is perceived as objects. The will is omnipresent and eternal, and thus it fully satisfies Parmenides's and Shankara's requirements. The urge, the will, is the creator of the world, and it is one with what is created. It is the true being, the primal reality. It is *what we are*.

CHAPTER 8

On Religion and the Perennial Philosophy

Adam: Do you know what I find striking, Hugo? That in our conversation we have covered many philosophical theories and religious ideas, but hardly discussed Christianity.

Hugo: That's an interesting observation that deserves a discussion. But let us first define what the nature of Christianity is, or better still, of religion in general. And here, first of all, the words of Schopenhauer come to mind: religion is truth allegorically and mythically expressed and so rendered attainable and digestible by mankind in general.[57] We began our conversation with the observation that knowledge is worthless if it remains theoretical and becomes effective only when we realise it as an immediate experience. Metaphors and myths are a way by which that abstract, theoretical knowledge can be made concrete and becomes an insight, becomes understanding. And this is the area of religion.

Adam: Give an example.

Hugo: Look at the myth of the original sin. Suffering, according to Christians, entered the world after Adam and Eve ate the fruit from the tree of the knowledge of good and evil. The first human couple was driven out of the Garden of Eden as a result, and eternal life was taken away from them. From then on, men have had to eat bread by the sweat of their faces, and women have had to give birth to children in pain. This is the myth. The truth behind that myth, however, is that 'there is something wrong about us as we naturally stand'; that this individual existence is not our real existence and that our true being is of a completely different nature. And that we ourselves are responsible for this state we are in, including the suffering we experience — as we have learned during this journey! But how much more accessible and vivid is the myth of the original sin than the arduous path we have had to travel to reach this understanding. Now, of course, the articulation of a metaphysical idea in myth, image and allegory occurs in other religions too; think of Hinduism for example, with its many colourful deities and myths. In fact, the very conception of God can be seen in this light. As Swami Vivekananda wrote, the average person cannot think about anything other than something concrete, and the same goes for spiritual ideas, ideas that most people can only grasp if they are reduced to his level. For this reason, many religions are theistic. The divine is conceived as something anthropomorphic: like a human being, but powerful, a kind of superman, omnipotent, omniscient, stripped of bad human characteristics but nevertheless a human being, and thus appealing and tangible.

Adam: How do you imagine that? That some religious leaders have thought: we know how things are, but the people are too stupid to understand, so let's make up a nice, appealing myth to make the truth understandable? Surely that seems unlikely and tends towards a conspiracy theory.

Hugo: I think speaking in metaphors and allegories often comes naturally when trying to convey an insight. Again, remember that understanding is not conceptual and therefore cannot be communicated by words alone. No, if you want to share a religious insight, myths and allegories are appropriate ways to do that. As Jesus himself said: 'Therefore speak I to them in parables: because they seeing see not; and hearing they hear not, neither do they understand.'[58] By the way, there are more abstract forms of Christianity where the allegorical, mythical element plays a lesser role. Christian mysticism, for example. But also Christian Gnosticism.

Adam: We've come across that last one before, but to be honest I don't know that much about it.

Hugo: Prior to a few decades ago, nobody did! Until then, our knowledge of the Gnostics was limited to what could be gathered from scattered fragments and from writings by opponents of the movement, such as the second-century Church Father Irenaeus of Lyon who in his work *Against Heresies* vehemently criticised the Gnostics. This remained the case until many centuries later, in 1945, an Egyptian farmer accidentally stumbled upon a collection of Gnostic texts dating from the first centuries AD near the town of Nag Hammadi in Egypt. Now Gnostics differ fundamentally from orthodox Christians in a number of ways. First, as the name gnosis — knowledge — suggests, for Gnostics it is knowledge, which should be understood as spiritual insight, that brings salvation. More precisely, insight into our true nature, into what we really are. In addition, Gnosticism holds that the world of time and space is not the true world but is illusory, or at least represents only a part of the real world. And finally, that part of our being, in fact the essential part, is identical with God. That knowing yourself at the deepest level is equivalent to knowing God.

Adam: Interesting parallels with our conclusions.

Hugo: I referred to them at the beginning of our conversation for a reason!

Adam: But, indeed, also fundamentally different from mainstream Christianity, whether Catholic or Protestant. I mean, for Christians, it is faith that brings salvation. And the world is not illusory, it is the creation of God himself. And it clearly goes against Christian doctrine to argue that we are identical with God. God is transcendent, not immanent!

Hugo: And these fundamentally different views therefore led in the first centuries of Christianity to a battle between what we now call the orthodox doctrine on the one hand, and Gnosticism on the other. A battle that the orthodox won, after which they wiped out almost all traces of the Gnostics. So the Gnostic works found in Egypt had likely been deliberately hidden there, probably by monks, after the orthodox Church had branded these works as heretical and called for their destruction. Which was thus almost successful, since apart from the Nag Hammadi writings, only a few loose fragments remained here and there. Now Elaine Pagels, author of the book *The Gnostic Gospels*,[59] has a fascinating and cogent explanation for the theological stance of orthodox Christianity. At the time of the fierce persecution of Christians and the desire to spread the faith, it was crucial to make this religion appeal to the widest possible audience. And you can't achieve that by linking salvation to an esoteric insight given to a few; but by linking it to faith it becomes attainable to the average person.

Adam: Interesting.

Hugo: But there are more positions of the church that relate to the turbulent times in which Christianity developed and the specific challenges that that emerging faith struggled with. The resurrection of Jesus, for example. In the gospels, so claims Pagels, it is not at all clear whether Jesus was resurrected in the body or as a spirit. But according to the orthodox view as it developed in the first centuries after Christ's death, there was no doubt about this: Jesus resurrected in the flesh after his crucifixion. Why? Because Christ's resurrection lends legitimacy to papal succession. The fact that Peter had been the first to see and be in personal contact with the resurrected Jesus lends authority to the claim that Jesus had put him in charge of the church after his resurrection, and thus to the papal succession.

There was also a debate between Gnostics and orthodox Christians as to whether Jesus was human, and suffered on the cross as a human being, or a divine, spiritual being, who could not suffer physically and thus did not suffer during his crucifixion. Why did the orthodox insist on the former? Because it gave Christians, during the time of fierce Christian persecution, confidence that by suffering and dying, they were following in the footsteps of Christ, that they could identify with Christ through their suffering. This gave strength to persecuted believers and motivated them to persevere in their faith. In short, Christianity, like other religions, is an interpretation of universal truth adapted to suit the psychological, intellectual, and social characteristics and needs of a particular period.

Adam: This is incredibly fascinating. This would show that religion is the work of mortals, heavily influenced by local and contemporary circumstances.

Hugo: This, by the way, entirely in line with the idea of a perennial philosophy, or perennialism.

Adam: Perennialism?

Hugo: This idea, popularised to some extent by Aldous Huxley, is that many religious and philosophical systems share the same truth, although expressed in different forms as an adaptation to the needs and characteristics of people in a particular period in history. Concretely, Christian mysticism, Islamic Sufism, Vedanta and other philosophies and movements in Hinduism, certain schools of Buddhism, and Gnosticism as well, essentially convey the same message. Namely that, as Huxley described it,

> [...] there is a Godhead, Ground, Brahman, Clear Light of the Void, which is the unmanifested principle of all manifestations. That the Ground is at once transcendent and immanent. That it is possible for human beings to love, know and, from virtually, to become actually identical with the divine Ground.[60]

Perennialism is the movement

> [...] that recognizes a divine Reality substantial to the world of things and lives and minds; the psychology that finds in the soul something similar to, or even identical with, divine Reality; the ethic that places man's final end in the knowledge of the immanent and transcendent Ground of all being [...].[61]

There is also a good description of perennialism in the book *Mysticism* by British writer F.C. Happold:

> This phenomenal world of matter and individual consciousness is only a partial reality and is the manifestation of a Divine Ground in which all partial realities have their being.[62]

Adam: We are not individual consciousness. We are not individuals, nor does our essence lie in consciousness. We are the will, the urge to spatial manifestation, like everything that exists in the universe. From the smallest particle to galaxies, from inanimate matter to living organisms — everything is essentially this will.

Hugo: And so Happold continues:

> It is of the nature of man that not only can he have knowledge of this Divine Ground by inference, but also he can realize it by direct

intuition, superior to discursive reason, in which the knower is in
some way united to the known.

Adam: The point is not to obtain discursive knowledge of this truth;
the essence is to turn it into an insight. From knowledge to understanding, which is what you started our conversation with.

Hugo: And then:

> The nature of man is not a single but a dual one. He has not one
> but two selves, the phenomenal ego, of which he is chiefly con-
> scious and which he tends to regard as his true self, and a non-phe-
> nomenal, eternal self, an inner man, the spirit, the spark of divinity
> within him, which is his true self. It is possible for a man, if he so
> desires and is prepared to make the necessary effort, to identify
> himself with his true self and so with the Divine Ground, which is
> of the same or like nature.

Adam: In this way, we can wake up from the dream, lose the decep-
tive and false sense of familiarity with ourselves and the world, and be
united with our true nature.

Hugo: Exactly. It is the purpose of life to identify ourselves with
this primal being, to whom all creation and decay are essentially alien:

> It is the chief end of man's earthly existence to discover and iden-
> tify himself with this true self. By so doing, he will come to an
> intuitive knowledge of the Divine Ground and so apprehend
> Truth as it really is, and not as to our limited human percep-
> tions it appears to be. Not only that, he will enter into a state of
> being which has been given different names, eternal life, salvation,
> enlightenment, etc.

Adam: I see significant overlaps with the conclusion of our journey.

Hugo: Schopenhauer would agree with you. In fact, he predated
the likes of Huxley, Happold, and even earlier thinkers like René
Guénon in introducing this idea of a perennial philosophy, albeit
without using that specific term. Schopenhauer, as I mentioned, saw
religion mainly as a mythical and allegorical vessel of a truth difficult

to grasp in its pure form; a vessel moreover, that is adapted to the particular circumstances of a time and place. As he wrote, 'the Indian, Christian, and Mohammedan mystics, quietists, and ascetics are different in every respect except in the inner meaning and spirit of their teachings'[63]. And he saw his own philosophy fully aligned with this inner meaning.

Adam: However, I also notice fundamental differences. Nowhere in the representatives of perennialism is the will mentioned. Let alone that this will is recognized as the ultimate reality, the thing-in-itself.

Hugo: On the face of it, that is indeed a huge contrast, I agree. For how different is a 'spark of divinity', or the 'Divine Ground', from the blind will we identified as the primal being. Not a God, not a heavenly being, but a blunt urge. Not even a will to life, something to which you could still attach something of value, but a will for manifestation in space, a goal that cannot stand the light of consciousness and must irrevocably result in its rejection. In Schopenhauer's words: nothing else can be stated as the aim of our existence except the knowledge that it would be better for us not to exist.[64] For not only must the goal seem meaningless to us, suffering is inherent to it. However we live our lives or organise society, the will remains a blind urge that will necessarily lead to struggle, suffering, old age, and death. The will that manifests itself in the organic and inorganic will always keep striving, because striving is its true essence that cannot be fulfilled by any achieved goal and thus cannot find final satisfaction. Like the life of a plant, which Schopenhauer so beautifully describes as a

> [...] restless, never satisfied striving, a ceaseless activity through higher and higher forms, till the final point, the seed, becomes anew a starting-point; and this repeated *ad infinitum*; nowhere there is a goal, nowhere a final satisfaction, nowhere a point of rest.[65]

The eternal pounding of the waves on the shore is an apt metaphor for the nature of the world: an eternal, restless pursuit with no end goal. This is why, for humans, happiness is so difficult to achieve. No satisfaction is lasting, and possession often means the end of enjoyment;

it is only the starting point of a new pursuit. 'The eye is not satisfied with seeing, nor the ear filled with hearing', says Ecclesiastes.[66] As Schopenhauer says, the incessant efforts to eliminate suffering have no other result than that suffering simply changes shape. Human life is therefore tossed back and forth between suffering and boredom, boredom which 'like a lurking bird of prey, falls upon every secure life.'[67] Not only does our existence consist of striving for something that must astonish and repulse us when we realise its nature, it is also marked by suffering and restlessness. This suffering is caused by what we can call the struggle for matter, that is, spatial manifestation; an important aspect of the will, namely that material forms seek to swallow up each other's matter, to integrate it into their own forms, something that we see so clearly in organic processes and that is the cause for nature being 'red in tooth and claw'. Each piece of matter, organic and inorganic, as it were sees itself as the centre of the universe and tries to draw all matter to itself.

Adam: The will is such a bizarre phenomenon, and moreover something that causes so much suffering, causing it *to itself* in fact, that one wonders: what is the reason that the will is like this? Why this restless striving, this suffering, this blind will?

Hugo: This, Adam, is an understandable question. But a meaningless one, however difficult that is for the mind to accept. You are asking why. This question implies that there is a ground for how the will is as it is. But as we discussed in relation to the freedom of the will: the will has no ground, and hence no explanation. The table here has a ground. It was put here by me, after I had it made. The fact that it is brown has a ground. Light of a certain frequency is reflected back, causing it to appear in my consciousness as brown. The fact that we are talking here has an explanation. But the will, as we already saw, is free, without ground. The will *is*. It is not something caused by something else, and therefore has no explanation. The question of why the will is, why the will is as it is, is therefore meaningless. The thing-in-itself is the will to manifest in space, and that is all we can say about it.

Adam: Yet it is claimed by many representatives of perennialism that understanding, realising this true nature, is accompanied by a kind of ecstatic feeling. And with none of these representatives is there any mention of the will as that which is found in the depths of our existence. In Buddhism, the will (in the form of desire) of course plays a major role, but not as a metaphysical concept, in my view. Explain that then, Hugo.

Hugo: Let me rephrase your question: if the will is our primal being, how come all these mystics don't recognise it as such? And also, how is it that experiencing our questionable nature, to say the least, leads to feelings of euphoria?

Adam: Exactly.

Hugo: Before I answer this, let me explain what 'salvation' means in the context of the will as ultimate reality and our true inner being. The relationship between insight into our true nature and salvation is that the former leads to the latter, in the sense that the will, this eternal, restless striving, transforms and is extinguished. You know that the will, the urge that we identified as the primal being of the cosmos, is blind. By nature, it does not know what it is. But the integral knowledge of the essence of the world acts as a sedative, or better still, as an extinguisher. When we realise what we are, this striving for manifestation in space with all the misery and pain that comes with it, this will is extinguished. I discussed this earlier: the will can, through insight into itself, transform itself. By which, incidentally, it also shows its free nature.

Adam: Could you say: we want certain situations, things, achieve specific goals, but we do not, that is, the will does not want itself when it sees itself in its totality?

Hugo: That's a good way of putting it. In fact, this is a more integral variant of understanding the ground for finding the opposite sex attractive, which we already discussed. If you recognise that those large breasts, those wide hips, represent the potential for strong, healthy offspring and that we *therefore* see them as beautiful, as attractive, then the spell breaks. Seeing the will in its totality in this way makes — or at least can make — the will retrace its steps and annul itself. The insight into the whole, into the inner nature of the thing-in-itself, Schopenhauer writes, goes to work as a quieter of all and every willing.[68]

Incidentally, on a smaller scale, art also acts as such a quieter. We saw earlier that art is communication of things that cannot be conveyed by words alone, by concepts; it is a form through which insights can be conveyed. And, according to Schopenhauer, good art shows us the essence of the world; the will, in other words. Beautiful paintings, poems and especially music express 'the innermost nature of all life and existence',[69] although this cannot be captured in concepts and is thus beyond our understanding.

Adam: So you could see the enjoyment of art as a fleeting, temporary salvation, but a salvation that is not accompanied by a rational understanding.

Hugo: Exactly. In fact, we can talk about four classes of knowledge and understanding. We discussed this briefly at the beginning. First of all, there is trivial knowledge: facts. Something that cannot help us understand what we are, or at best in an indirect way. Then you have philosophical knowledge. For example, 'the world is my representation'. Knowledge that we can learn, communicate and discuss, but remains worthless if it is not accompanied by insight, by understanding. Then there is insight that can still be expressed in words, although words alone, in the form of concepts, cannot convey this insight. This is actually where we ended up: the philosophical insight that we are the will, an understanding gained through careful introspection, coupled with extrapolation and generalisation. And then, as a fourth class, there is the insight through art: an insight that flies below the radar of knowledge, cannot be captured in concepts and cannot be expressed in words. An insight that can temporarily extinguish the will, although the perceiver does not understand how and why!

Adam: So our path led to the understanding of that third class.

Hugo: Right, the philosophical understanding of what we are. And this insight can quench that will, transform the urge we always feel and experience. It is this extinguishing of the will that leads to the feeling of ecstasy. As if a pressure falls away; a feeling of relief, as if ropes that bound you to the earth are suddenly cut loose. This feeling is somewhat similar to what you experience when a disturbing noise suddenly disappears, a noise you only really became aware of the moment it vanished. This state is characterised by what the writer and mystic Romain Rolland calls the 'oceanic feeling': a sense of eternal life, a mystical experience of being one with the world. Through this experience, the exile who thought himself an individual returns home. We are the One and All, the primal being, the Absolute, Brahman, or if you like, God. *Tat tvam asi.* This is known among the various representatives of perennialism as final emancipation, moksha, nirvana, salvation, enlightenment, et cetera. But again, this feeling, this state of will-less ecstasy is the result of this insight, not identical with it. Through insight, you can experience this ecstasy, but there are other ways to reach this enlightenment, apart from the temporary enlightenment through art that we just discussed.

The Indians were more aware than anyone else that there are several paths leading to salvation, and these paths are known as the different yogas. Jnana yoga, for example, is the path of knowledge, albeit a different path from the one we have followed (also among the Indians, the will never played a major role, let alone that it was identified as Brahman). In this path, realisation of the true self is gained through meditation and reflection, often with the help of a guru. In addition, there are paths that can lead to enlightenment that are not based on insight or knowledge, but on suppressing the small self: the I we so falsely associate ourselves with. Suppressing this individual makes room for the realisation of our true being: 'The breaking down of the little self and the building up of the Real Self', as Swami Vivekananda called it. As Huxley put it, 'the more there is of the self, the less there is of the Godhead': denying the small self opens up the possibility of the experience of oneness with Brahman, with the thing-in-itself. Karma yoga is the path of egoless action, the performance of labour without being attached to personal consequences, acting without self-interest. Bhakti yoga is the path of devotion to the supreme, a love for God to supplant the love for and attachment to the small self. All these are ways of suppressing the false little self to make way for our true nature and thereby lead to this oceanic feeling, to becoming one with the One, our true being, in a state of ecstatic will-lessness.

Adam: But this does not need to be accompanied by insight into our true nature.

Hugo: Exactly. Again, knowledge of the will can work as a quieter of the will, but as you yourself pointed out, in almost none of the representatives of perennialism is the will associated with the core of our being. In large part, that is because among these representatives, salvation was attained by means of other paths than that of knowledge, such as the path of devotion, also familiar to Christians of course, or the path of selfless labour.

Adam: Or asceticism.

Hugo: Asceticism, celibacy, right down to self-flagellation: all ways of self-denial, methods of letting the little ego die off to make room for the realisation of our true nature. In the words of Jesus, 'He who loves his life loses it; but he who hates his life in this world will preserve it for eternal life.'[70] This denial of the small self is therefore the basis of many moral virtues in both Christianity and Eastern religions. This is also why so much value is placed on suffering in many faiths, as it can be a trigger to turn away from life and the illusion of the small self. The monk Swami Rama Tirtha called poverty blessed, as it would form a 'ladder to the throne of God'. Schopenhauer called purification through suffering 'the next best course' after the path of knowledge (the latter he considered only attainable for a small number of people).[71] But the reverse is also true. Material well-being strengthens the small self and obscures the path to discovering our true nature. This is also why, according to legend, Buddha's father surrounded his son in his palace with luxury and shielded him from illness, old age, pain, and death in the hope that he would not choose a spiritual path. And this is also why, in times of abundance and prosperity, people have less need for religion, for metaphysical explanations. 'God isn't compatible with machinery and scientific medicine and universal happiness', as Huxley wrote in *Brave New World*. Or, as Jesus said, 'it is easier for a camel to go through the eye of a needle, than for a rich man to enter into the kingdom of God.'[72]

There is thus a difference between means to salvation and all the behaviours that follow from this experience. Different things, but often identical in form. For example, sexual abstinence is seen as a means towards enlightenment, but also a manifestation of it; in an enlightened state, there are no sexual desires. It is, in other words, possible to allow the will to die off, to suppress the individual, allowing you to enter a state where these things are part of your natural state. In the words of Thomas à Kempis, 'where heavenly grace and true charity enter in, there neither envy nor narrowness of heart nor self-love will have place, there is no more envy and no more constriction of heart, nor shall self-love seize you.'[73]

Adam: But then the question still remains why, in all these representatives of the perennial philosophy, in all these descriptions of moments of enlightenment, no reference is made to the will. I mean, you are one with that will, according to you that which we essentially are, and one doesn't recognise it even in enlightenment? Those things don't seem to be reconcilable to me. The Vedantists, whom you often quoted, see the thing-in-itself as something fundamentally different — as a kind of supreme subject, a cosmic awareness, as 'pure consciousness'.

Hugo: Indeed, we already discussed that many Vedantists describe Brahman as *sat-chit-ananda* — truth-consciousness-bliss. Vivekananda described that as the highest concept of God still comprehensible by humans. There is no better, more accurate description of Brahman, according to him.

Adam: That seems far removed from the will.

Hugo: It is indeed far removed from our findings if we see *sat-chit-ananda* as a description of Brahman. But some Vedantists suggest we should interpret it differently: not as a description of Brahman itself, but as a description of the *subjective experience* of Brahman as the ultimate unchanging reality. And in this manner, it is compatible with the conclusions of our discussion.

Adam: How?

Hugo: *Sat-chit-ananda* can be seen as a description of the experience of will-lessness, the blissful feeling associated with the extinguishing of the will. At the same time, this experience does not provide insight into the nature of that will. You have to keep in mind that all experience, all insight, by definition involves consciousness. Consciousness is implicit to it, so too to this experience. But that does not mean that consciousness is a property of the will per se! Besides, this experience concerns the *extinction* of the will, not the will as it is blindly active in the world. And with this experience ('consciousness') comes the oceanic feeling ('bliss'), and the awareness of the dissolution of the individual into the One and All ('truth'). But we would be making a mistake if we were to regard this experience of truth-consciousness- bliss as the thing-in-itself. The *experience* of the *transformation* of the will does not give *knowledge* of the will as it is by nature.

Adam: Because that knowledge can only be obtained from our experience as acting, knowing individuals! Fascinating.

Hugo: Indeed. Incidentally, there are descriptions of Brahman that are closer to our idea of the thing-in-itself. For instance, the Indologist and philosopher Paul Deussen, a scholar of Schopenhauer's philosophy and a personal friend of Swami Vivekananda, described Brahman as a creative principle realising itself in the world. Which is very close to our description of the will as the thing-in-itself.

Adam: And what about the will in Buddhism?

Hugo: When discussing Buddhism, it is important to realise that there are many schools of this religion, and it is therefore challenging if not impossible to give a precise and unequivocal definition of its teaching. But undoubtably the will, in the meaning of our cravings and desires, plays an important role. According to the Four Noble Truths, our cravings (*tanha*) are seen as the cause of suffering (*dukkha*). But, as you rightly said, in Buddhism the will does not have the same metaphysical import as it has in Schopenhauer's philosophy, let alone that it is positioned as the core of our self or that of the world. In fact, according to the doctrine of *anatta*, the very the idea of an unchanging, permanent self is denied. Moreover, in Buddhism our cravings and desires are often seen as a consequence of this false conception of ourselves, or of ignorance in general. We, of course, consider this will to be primary, not as a consequence of any conception or any other mental activity, which also explains the working of this will in unconscious and inanimate phenomena, which Buddhism is not able to do well (but, should be added, does also not aspire to do. Focusing on orthopraxy, on correct conduct, this doctrine is mostly limited to man and how to free himself).

Adam: But going back to the transformation of the will, the will in our definition. If the will has extinguished itself in a state of enlightenment, can you still talk about the will? If the will has stopped willing, what did it become?

Hugo: That, Adam, is beyond the limits of the knowable. Knowledge is the result of a cognitive activity that no longer exists in this state of being. And so also the language that is so closely intertwined with this mind is no longer able to articulate it. What we ultimately find when we descend to that level is simply not intelligible. In Koestler's words, 'logical reasoning gradually loses its compass value as the mind approaches the magnetic pole of Truth or the Absolute'.[74]

Adam: We started our conversation with the superiority of insight and understanding over knowledge. But you're saying here that in the depths of our existence, knowledge has become powerless and impotent?

Hugo: Indeed. All religions, as Schopenhauer stated,

> [...] at their highest point end in mysticism and mysteries, that is to say, in darkness and veiled obscurity. These really indicate merely a blank spot for knowledge, the point where all knowledge necessarily ceases.[75]

That is why the descriptions of our true nature given by mystics are so vague. Let us also remember how we identified the will as our true being: through introspection and then through generalisations and extrapolations, we identified the will as that which also lies behind other phenomena — unconscious processes, evolution, physical forces and even matter itself. This philosophical method - where one, as Schopenhauer put it, starts from *without* - brought us to understand our nature as the will. But 'knowing' no longer exists in the state of enlightenment, besides the fact that, as we already saw, in that state of enlightenment that very will is extinguished, has transformed itself. What we find in this experience is not apprehensible by the mind, and so it can no longer be described in language. This is the realm of the mystic, who, contrary to the philosopher, starts from *within*.[76]

Adam: And there experiences the unspeakable Divine Ground.

Hugo: Exactly. It is an understanding that belongs to our earlier defined fourth class of knowledge and insight where also art was placed: an insight, or perhaps better, a realisation that goes beyond knowledge. It is therefore that the Christian mystic Meister Eckhart said: 'Why dost thou prate of God? Whatever thou sayest of Him is untrue'. How Schopenhauer put it, here 'we lack concepts for what the will now is; indeed, we lack all data for such concepts. We can only describe it as that which is free to be or not to be the will-to-live'.[77]

Adam: Fascinating. And this shows, indeed, how closely aligned Schopenhauer's philosophy is with the perennial philosophy.

Hugo: Indeed. And it's highly unfortunate that this hasn't been recognised by later thinkers as Schopenhauer's teachings form a solid philosophical foundation for mystical doctrines. For example, Huxley doesn't even mention Schopenhauer in his works, despite the profound similarities in their ideas.

Adam: But still, going back to the idea of salvation. Doesn't this idea contradict the findings of our journey? After all, we had just figured out that we are not the individual, but the will. Now the idea of salvation among representatives of perennialism seems to assume the salvation of the individual. Whether it is escaping from the cycle of death and rebirth, or being absorbed into a Divine Ground, the individual is what finds redemption. But at the same time, we are told we are not the individual; the individual is an illusion. In our case, what we really are is the will. Therefore, shouldn't salvation be seen more as a local, limited extinction? An individual may be redeemed, but the world keeps on turning and the will continues to strive in countless other people, plants, animals, and inanimate objects. Thus, the idea of salvation assumes the same false identification of our being with the individual. In this respect, redemption solves the problem of existence as effectively as suicide: it eliminates an individual manifestation of the will, but this will continue to blindly strive elsewhere.

Hugo: You have a point here, Adam. The extinguishing of the will in ascetics, saints and seers has not extinguished the will everywhere and forever. The will has transformed itself in, or perhaps you should say, through these individuals, but it continues to manifest itself blindly in countless other individuals, life forms and material phenomena, despite these 'local extinctions', as you so eloquently put it.

Adam: Does that mean there is no hope? That suffering is eternal and insurmountable? That the waves will continue to pound on the shore in perpetuity?

Hugo: These are good questions, which may not have satisfactory answers, I'm afraid. But we can say a bit more about them. First, one can question whether there is suffering without consciousness. As we saw, there was manifestation in space before there was life, let alone consciousness. Could you talk about suffering then? Yes, there was struggle, in the sense that will manifestations in space were competing with each other, trying to swallow up each other's matter in their own forms. But perhaps suffering only appeared with the emergence of consciousness, most notably in the form of pain. In that case, as Schopenhauer wrote, 'it would be much better if, on the earth as little as on the moon, the sun were able to call forth the phenomena of life; and if, here as there, the surface were still in a crystalline state.'[78]

Adam: Then, destroying sentient beings would be a kind of redemption? A bit of a wry conclusion.

Hugo: I agree. But another possibility is that on a cosmic scale, there is a moment, an end point where the will does find peace. We assume here with Schopenhauer that the will is eternal and restless, has no end point and therefore can never find satisfaction. But perhaps this is also an outdated view, similar to the pre-evolutionary *Weltanschauung* in the biological realm. For evolutionary thinking also made its appearance in cosmology in the form of the Big Bang theory: the idea that the universe arose from a hot point of infinite density and high temperature. Is our pursuit of spatial manifestation, the creation of an ever-increasing hierarchical order, related to this? Are we perhaps striving to return to that point of perfect order, of unity? Is that the goal of striving, and will we — the will — eventually find peace there? Interestingly, we find similar speculations in Edgar Allan Poe's work *Eureka*:

> The constitution [of the material universe, JPvR] is effected
> by forcing the originally and therefore normally One into the
> abnormal condition of Many. An action of this character implies
> reaction. A diffusion from Unity, under the conditions, involves
> a tendency to return into Unity — a tendency ineradicable until
> satisfied.

Adam: So maybe our being is not an ocean, but a river. And we individuals are like little waves in this river, without us knowing where
this river flows…

Hugo: A nice elaboration of the metaphor, but this idea must
of course remain speculative. Nor should we forget the nature of the
method we applied in our quest, and with it, its limitations. Through
introspection, we have gained insight into ourselves and then,
through generalisations and extrapolations, identified the will as that
which also lies behind other phenomena — unconscious processes,
evolution, physical forces and matter itself. But with Schopenhauer,
we have to conclude that our method of getting to know ourselves
and the thing-in-itself sticks to

> […] the actual facts of outward and inward experience as they are
> accessible to everyone, and shows their true and deepest connex-
> ion, yet without really going beyond them to any extramundane
> things, and the relations of these to the world.[79]

In our — empirical — method of understanding our nature and that
of the world, we are bound by knowledge and insight that are derived
from our experiences. And we have come a long way with this: we
have identified our will as the essence behind basically all phenomena
that are part of our experiences, from the organic to the inorganic,
from the astronomical to the subatomic. But with that, of course,
we cannot rule out that there are things beyond the scope of our
experience and knowledge, in addition to the knowledge of the extinguished will which we concluded earlier as beyond reach. Perhaps
there is an order that explains the origin of will, that sheds light on
why things are as they are, but is fundamentally beyond the scope of

our knowing. In other words, we have solved the riddle of the world insofar as it is within reach of human knowledge.

Adam: And knowledge was not our strong suit anyway, which is why it takes us so much effort to discover our true nature, and find out what we really are…

Hugo: We cannot repeat this enough: we naturally have no idea of what we really are and are not even aware of it. Think of the fact that the greatest thinkers have been able to step over the greatest mystery, which is what we ourselves are, and that it is only through tricky, difficult paths that it is possible to discover this, where, moreover, it is only those with the right attention, focus and imagination who can complete the journey. And then, having completed it, we cannot even be sure what there might be beyond our reach. But let us not forget what we *did* discover through our method of introspection, Adam. That having thrown overboard the persistent and deep-rooted misconceptions about our nature, we recognise that we are one with the will, this urge for spatial manifestation, for realisation in space. That this is the One and All, the reality behind all individual phenomena. A knowledge that, when it sinks in as insight, solves great philosophical and ethical problems, not in the least those of mortality and of evil and suffering. No, we were never born and never die: we are the kernel of the universe that always was and always will be. We are our maker and creator, and the evil and suffering of the world is our own creation, an eternal justice where perpetrator and victim are in fact one, and we always get what we deserve in the end. Life, which must necessarily strike any objective observer as a bizarre and cruel phenomenon, is thus explained. The questions, in the words of the poet Leopardi,

> […] for what intent
> Our race was born, and why so loaded down
> With grief and misery; to what last goal
> Nature and fate are driving us, and who
> Derives delight or profit from our pain;
> How ruled, how ordered, to what issue moves
> This strange creation sages heap with praise
> And I am satisfied to wonder at.

have been answered.[80] But, as he continues, '...truth, once known, though sad, has its delight'. On an intellectual level, but especially when this insight leads to the mystical oceanic feeling, when the will extinguishes itself and the individual dissolves into the One and All. Perhaps not an eternal salvation, since, as far as we can see, the will continues to strive on, like the waves of the sea will always beat against the shore. But still, a welcome moment of calm in the storm of existence.

CHAPTER 9

On Politics, Ideology, and the Future

Adam: My view of life has indeed changed fundamentally, Hugo. It is as you told me at the beginning of our journey: what we are, and its relation to the brain, the body, our will, the world, even our idea of individuality which we so much associate with our identity: everything is totally, fundamentally different. As you said, everyone is living in a dream, only the philosopher strives to wake up. And which of us is really awake?

Hugo: Not everyone is interested in philosophy, and even fewer have the luxury of being able to immerse themselves into it. And only a small proportion of those come to adhere to Schopenhauer's ideas. Besides, let us not forget that Schopenhauer's actual influence is smaller than his popularity. He did influence another famous German philosopher, Friedrich Nietzsche, and still inspires thinkers, artists, and writers to this day. His erratic, eccentric behaviour also earned him a kind of cult status. But nevertheless, his actual metaphysics is far less influential. Although he is still considered relevant as a thinker about the human condition, about man and his place the world, his metaphysical system is considered out of date. Many people know Schopenhauer, may also appreciate him for his beautiful style of writing and his apt description of the miserable sides of life, but that does not mean that people have accepted his message that the will is the essence of man and the universe. Indeed, after his death, the movement that strongly emerged in his time and which he so vehemently opposed, naturalism, has only become more dominant. Nor have other representatives of the perennial philosophy been able to gain a foothold in the West since his time, although they certainly experienced periods of popularity. For instance, the influential theosophical movement of the late 19th century drew upon Neoplatonism, Hinduism, and Buddhism. Then around 1900, there was an interesting phenomenon of Indian monks who preached in the West, including Swami Vivekananda and Swami Rama Tirtha who I mentioned earlier, which gained significant popularity and engaged with prominent intellectuals of that time. Aldous Huxley was a regular visitor to the Vedanta Society of Southern California and befriended another Indian philosopher, Jiddu Krishnamurti. Interestingly, interest among intellectuals in Eastern philosophy seemed to wane in the 1960s when its influence on popular culture increased (think of the Bhagwan movement, Hare Krishna, et cetera). Today, Buddhism and meditation techniques such as mindfulness are very popular, but one can question whether one can speak of a large, widely perceived influence on our culture.

Adam: And Christianity? What's left of that?

Hugo: That's a good question. Schopenhauer, despite the many flaws he saw in that faith, had a great appreciation for Christianity. For him, its essence was its exhortation to self-denial and resignation — the denial of the will, in other words. Like all representatives of perennialism, Christianity preaches that our earthly life is not our true destiny and that the denial of the flesh — the will — brings salvation.

Adam: You seem to suggest that self-denial is essential to Christianity, but that is not true. It is by no means preached in all Christian branches.

Hugo: That is true, and Schopenhauer could therefore not find himself in agreement with all Christian traditions. For instance, he saw Protestantism, which places much less emphasis on self-denial (and in line with this does not demand celibacy for the clergy), as a degeneration, a breaking away from the essence of the Christian faith. Schopenhauer viewed Luther's attacks on asceticism, for example through his rejection of monasticism (which Schopenhauer called a 'methodical denial of the will, practised in common for the purpose of mutual encouragement'[81]), as an attack on the heart of Christianity.

Adam: But whether Catholic or Protestant, the Western world has become increasingly secularised since his time, a process that accelerated in the last decades. One wonders if the West can still be called Christian.

Hugo: And this has not been without consequences. You know that the West experiences a time of major, disruptive developments: large migratory flows and, as a result, huge demographic changes, the expansion of Islam, the rise of wokeism and the rising power of China, to name perhaps the most prominent. Above all, I see these developments as signs of a weakening of what is called Western civilisation: the culture that played a dominant role on the world stage economically, culturally, and militarily for about a thousand years. Since roughly the second half of the twentieth century, the West has been experiencing a decline in global dominance, initially evident in Europe and later followed by the United States (after its brief period of global hegemony).

Adam: Why is that, in your view? People sometimes refer to the two world wars of the 20th century as traumas that undermined the West's standing and, probably more importantly, its self-confidence.

Hugo: No doubt that has played a role in Europe, but it can't explain the decline of the United States. Without doubt, many factors play a role, including financial and economic, but the decline of the West, in my view, cannot be separated from secularisation. Which, by the way, I see as inevitable and the result of an inherent weakness of religion. As we discussed: religion is an allegorical and mythical expression of a philosophical truth. But with this, as Schopenhauer rightly said, it is both true and false. And the weakness of religions is that they cannot be overtly, but only covertly allegorical. If it is admitted that dogmas should not be taken literally, they lose their power. But the myths and allegories of Christianity no longer suffice. Discoveries in science have made belief in the Christian system untenable. The idea of a heaven and hell to which our souls would move after we die, the creation of the world by God (let alone in seven days), and the resurrection of Jesus after his crucifixion — all these are no longer credible or plausible to the modern mind. As Schopenhauer put it: mankind outgrows religion like a child's dress,[82] and, expressed in the terminology of perennialism, Christianity no longer meets the psychological, intellectual, and social characteristics and demands of our time. And unfortunately, the baby — the spiritual truth behind the faith — is thrown out with the bathwater — the myths and allegories that express this truth.

But, according to Schopenhauer, Christianity faces an additional handicap. While the teachings of Jesus align with the tradition of perennialism and, in Schopenhauer's view, were likely influenced by the East, in Christianity they are grafted onto the stem of Jewish theism found in the Old Testament. However, these are spiritually alien to each other: the will-denying doctrine of Jesus, which views life as our own responsibility and something to be conquered, contrasts with the belief in the good, omniscient creator of the Jews. In this perspective, life is inherently good, and our existence is beyond our responsibility. Mythically, this is resolved by the fall of Adam and Eve, by which mankind became responsible for its suffering and misery after all. But the forced and contrived nature of this myth explains, as Schopenhauer put it, why 'the Christian mysteries have obtained an appearance so strange and so opposed to common sense'.[83]

Whatever the exact reason and how various causes may interact, it is, in my view, evident that Christianity is on its last legs. And these developments at the spiritual level have far-reaching consequences on society as well. Christianity has to a considerable extent determined the norms and values of the West and, alongside classical civilisation, is an important pillar of Western culture. Christianity defined our view of life, suffering and death, and gave Western man his place in the universe. With the disappearance of religion, the spiritual basis of our culture has disappeared, and this alienated us from it. And with this, the strength and confidence to defend that culture also vanished. For how can a non-Christian be expected to understand the Christian world sufficiently to value it, love it, let alone muster the requisite will and strength to defend it? In this respect, living in the West without the Christian faith is like living in a building whose purpose we no longer quite understand, without remembering to whom or what we owe it, or why we should maintain it. Sometimes the disappearance of this spiritual pillar leads not only to doubt and lack of self-confidence, but to contempt and even hatred for one's own culture. As Swami Vivekananda put it, 'the mainspring of the strength of every race lies in its spirituality, and the death of that race begins on the day that spirituality wanes and materialism gains ground.'[84] Or, as the Colombian philosopher Nicolás Gómez Dávila said, 'cultures dry out when their religious ingredients evaporate'. In addition, the problem is not just that Christianity is disappearing; more than that, nothing substantial has replaced it. In practice, secularisation also means the disappearance of a general, broad-based spirituality, and with it the rise of its inevitable counterpart, materialism and hedonism. But no culture, no morality, and hence no civilisation can be built on the latter.

Adam: Secularisation is not only making our old civilisation vanish, but with the disappearance of spirituality, the hope of the emergence of a new one is also fading.

Hugo: At the very least, it doesn't make it any easier. But there is another important social effect of the demise of Christianity. In today's society, many people seem to be looking to compensate for the disappearance of our faith with surrogate goals such as saving the world from the supposedly destructive effects of climate change: efforts that recall religion in their pomposity, their idea of human guilt and sacrifice, eschatological visions of the end of time, and the ambition to change every aspect of our lives. You often find those religious sentiments in ambitions 'to make the world a better place', to use the cliche. As the British philosopher John Gray explains in his work *Seven Types of Atheism*:

> Life without any power that can secure order or some kind of ultimate justice is a frightening and for many an intolerable prospect. In the absence of such a power, human events could be finally chaotic, and no story could be told that satisfied the need for meaning. Struggling to escape this vision, atheists have looked for surrogates of the God they have cast aside.[85]

Incidentally, I think the loss of this justice might have had an even deeper impact on people than the loss of meaning. As we discussed earlier, life is characterised by imperfections: old age, disease, and death. Struggle and war. But also by hierarchical structures and, as a result, inequality between people, peoples and countries, an inequality that defies our sense of justice. Life is imperfect, and evil often seems to rule the world.

Adam: We started our conversation with it. And here, the insight arises, as William James put it, 'that there is something wrong about us as we naturally stand'.

Hugo: That is the essence. These imperfections are an indication that something is not right with existence as we experience it. And it is human nature not to accept that, but to seek an explanation, and ultimately a solution for it. This is the great, driving force behind the emergence not only of Christianity, but of all religions. In our conversation, we found an explanation for this imperfection at the metaphysical level: underlying the world is a blind will, an urge that necessarily leads to struggle, suffering, and death. The will that reveals itself in the organic and inorganic always continues to strive, because striving is its essence and cannot find final satisfaction, as far as we can see: nowhere an ultimate goal, nowhere rest. The idea that the world is imperfect, and we must therefore be redeemed from it, that our true destiny lies beyond this brief, individual existence, is shared by most religions and certainly by the representatives of perennialism. By acting in the morally correct way (for example by suppressing the self, or gaining insight into our true nature), we can be saved from the world and find eternal life in heaven, reach nirvana, or escape from the cycle of birth and death. But without God and without heaven, without a world above or beyond, this explanation must be sought within that world itself.

Adam: In what way then? By means of society not being properly arranged and organised?

Hugo: Exactly. And as a consequence, the solution would lie in social or political reform. 'Impose the right kind of organizations upon human beings, and all their problems, from sin and unhappiness to nationalism and war, will automatically disappear', as Huxley described this view.[86] The 20th century witnessed the dramatic consequences of this idea, a century in which, as Jordan Peterson put it, 'in the aftermath of God's death [...] the great collective horrors of communism and fascism sprang'.[87] Fascism, especially in the form of National Socialism, was an ideology that saw the solution to problems primarily in the cleansing of society of undesirable racial, cultural, and economic elements, after which utopia would dawn. This movement is responsible for perhaps the most heinous and evil phenomenon humanity has ever produced: the Holocaust. However, other ideologies should also be seen in this light. Communism, as you know, is rooted in the philosophy of Karl Marx, who in turn built on the ideas of Georg Wilhelm Friedrich Hegel who, as is well known, was scorned by his contemporary Schopenhauer. For Marx, the distribution of capital was a fundamental cause of social problems. Capital, he argued, is concentrated among a small group of people, and this group, in what he called a class struggle, seeks to maintain and increase its advantageous economic power structures. The solution, according to him, was a structural redistribution of capital, which would end inequality and exploitation. Indeed, the demise of capitalism would cure us once and for all of humanity's age-old woes. It is thus no coincidence that, as French sociologist and philosopher Raymond Aron noted, communism developed at a time when the spiritual vitality and authority of the church was waning.[88]

Adam: On the other hand, it's undeniable that some of Marx's ideas were indeed correct. Capital does have a tendency to accumulate. Just look at the state of the global economy today, with its billionaires and multinational companies wielding immense power due to their accumulated wealth. And many world events can be traced back to the influence of money. As the saying goes, money makes the world go round.

Hugo: But the main problem with Marx, in my view, lies not in the fact that he identified mechanisms that were incorrect: capital indeed tends to behave in the way he identified and has a powerful influence over society. The main issue with Marx is that he painted an oversimplified picture of reality; that he traced too much back to economic mechanisms and class struggle, ignoring many other, often more deeper mechanisms and motivations that are at work in society and drive human beings – such as those rooted in basic biological principles! How much in the world is not driven by man's

striving to simply survive and procreate? More than we perhaps wish
to admit, as we discussed earlier. It is moreover both simplistic and
cynical to reduce phenomena such as art, philosophy, literature, and
other esteemed cultural expressions to mere instruments of power
structures. Marx's simplification that also reveals itself on the moral
level by the way, classifying the proletariat as per definition good, and
capitalists as evil.

Adam: So, once again, the tendency of our mind to oversimplify
and overgeneralize rears its ugly head.

Hugo: Exactly! An additional, cardinal mistake in Marx's reasoning, of course, was the promise of utopia. Just look at the colossal failure of the communist experiment. Estimates suggest that 100 million
people died as a direct result of this system: an amount of human life
beyond imagination.[89] Jordan Peterson called the communist experiment the most terrible thing that happened in the 20th century (and
said that the fact that people are not fully aware of it today is a painful
testament to the decay of the education system).[90] But there are more
variations on this Marxist theme, variations that have asserted themselves strongly in recent years and have, like a contagious virus, spread
with an astonishing speed in the West. The so-called woke movement and critical race theory claim that many aspects of Western
culture are designed for white, Western man to maintain his power
and subjugate the rest of the world, with colonialism, slavery, and the
oppression of women being the most prominent examples. Race and
gender, for example, would not be rooted in biology, but be socially
constructed labels used to oppress non-whites and women.

Adam: So the oppressed proletarians of the communists gave way
to other groups.

Hugo: Right. And the behaviour of these oppressed would
be the result of this culture imposed by power structures, which
makes criminals victims of circumstances rather than responsible
for their own actions. Thus, Western culture is claimed to be fundamentally sexist and 'institutionally' racist. The solution to the problem would therefore lie in breaking down and 'decolonising' this
patriarchal Western culture, such as the traditional family, Christianity, civic values, capitalism, science, and rationality in general,

down to language and history. But like previous sweeping cultural revolutions, should it succeed it will equally end in deception, if not worse. Radical social reforms will never bring heaven on earth. Instead, they will generally cause only more misery because they upset a shaky balance in a complex social system of traditions, customs and trust often built up over hundreds of years, after which chaos, violence and arbitrariness often follow. The true explanation for life's imperfections and incongruities does not lie in a flawed social organisation or political system (although these can make life a lot more unpleasant). The true explanation is deeper, more fundamental, and the consequence, mythically speaking, of the curse acquired by Adam and along with him by the whole race, as Schopenhauer puts it.[91]

Adam: Suffering is inherent in life, inherent to an imperfect and flawed world. And the solution therefore lies not within the world, but beyond it.

Hugo: Indeed. Schopenhauer shows us what the real cause of suffering, inequality and injustice is and why these can never disappear through social change. Interestingly, even though many of the aforementioned revolutionary movements had not yet reached maturity in Schopenhauer's time, he was already warning against them. For instance, he speaks of 'demagogues' who shift all the blame for the world's glaring malfunctions onto governments and argue that if only they would do their part, heaven would exist on earth.[92]

Adam: But as Popper said, 'those who promise us paradise on earth never produced anything but a hell.'

Hugo: Yes, we cannot say we were not warned. But other elements of Schopenhauer's teaching could also have saved us from the misery of the twentieth century. For the idea that society is engineerable is built on the assumption that it is intelligible; that man has the intellectual abilities to have full knowledge of the world and to be able to oversee the consequences of actions and changes.

Adam: You already started our conversation with the observation that man's intellectual capacity tends to be grossly overrated.

Hugo: We saw that knowledge does not necessarily lead to an understanding of our true nature, but in addition, the ability to acquire knowledge is far less well developed than is commonly thought, something we have encountered many times in our conversation. What is knowledge? An important part consists of abstract concepts. Concepts are formed by abstracting essential or distinctive characteristics of individual things, which can then be communicated through language. Think of concepts like tree, house, or body: terms that encompass a vast array of individual phenomena, formed on the basis of shared, distinctive features while ignoring irrelevant ones. To appreciate the ability to form concepts and determine its scope, we must remember what it was created for. Above all, this must be seen within the context of the purpose of consciousness as such — to understand the world around us so that the will can respond to it. The mind has therefore evolved primarily to understand the natural world, for instance to know which plants are nutritious, which animals are dangerous, when to expect rain. So, it has not evolved at all to understand something as complex as a society, or to fathom the human mind. This explains Huxley's observation that the mind has a strong tendency for oversimplification, overgeneralisation, and over-abstraction. Although it is extremely useful for understanding relatively simple matters, it is not equipped to grasp more complex things, and it often errs when forming concepts by not being able to identify the right (essential, distinctive) features of phenomena. Oversimplification also exhibits itself in the tendency of man to falsely reduce complex systems to simple causal relations.

But even ignoring the underestimation of the complexity of systems, the human mind has great difficulty with determining the cause and effect as such. The idea that things happen as a result of causes is deeply rooted in our consciousness, but determining *what* exactly is the cause of certain events within complex reality is difficult for our minds to establish. Often cause and effect are mixed up, and in other cases, there is only correlation where a causal relationship is assumed. It is this weakness in human cognition that, according to renowned anthropologist J.G. Frazer, is the cause of belief in magic among primitive peoples.

Adam: Magic? Please define that term.

Hugo: For Frazer, magic is the idea that reality can be manipulated on the basis of contact (contagious magic) or equality (homeopathic magic). An example of the former is the use of a person's hair or nails with the intention of causing them harm, based on the fact that these body parts once belonged to that person. An example of homeopathic magic is performing an enactment of a hunt so that the actual hunt will be successful or inducing rain by sprinkling water on the ground. The fatal error of magic lies not in the general assumption of a lawful sequence of events, but in the total misconception of the nature of the laws governing that sequence. The pervasive nature of magic among primitive peoples, described in detail in Frazer's fascinating classic from 1890 *The Golden Bough*, is indicative of this weakness in the human mind. It is only by consistently and scrupulously following the scientific method that we come to know the true relationship of cause and effect and the natural laws involved.

Adam: A method that has undeniably led to impressive results, Hugo. Surely there is no denying that.

Hugo: Certainly, natural science has achieved an awful lot and has vastly increased our knowledge of the world. The application of this science in the form of technology testifies daily to its success and validity. But the history of science also shows that gaining knowledge of the physical and biological world — where science can really boast of great successes, though there is a lot that falls outside its scope — has not been an easy path. Almost everything we once thought and assumed to be real has eventually turned out to be wrong or had to be significantly modified. As Koestler puts it, 'in such crooked ways does the tree of science grow'. And don't forget, even in these modern times, superstition still lurks everywhere: for instance, there are whole scores of people today who dare not walk under a ladder.

Adam: Or who knock on wood for luck. You have a point there.

Hugo: And there is another notable weakness of the human mind, one that we also touched upon earlier. The way people view and interpret the world is rigid, inflexible, and difficult to adjust. Once people have classified the world into certain concepts, notions, and explanations, they will not be able to see and interpret the world differently. The phenomenon called tunnel vision, the reluctance to consider alternatives to one's preferred line of thought, is a consequence of this rigidity. When searching for the correct interpretation of a set of observations, people tend to see all clues from one hypothesis assumed to be correct, thus overlooking other explanations. This inflexibility of thinking also plagues science, and it explains why scientists analyse and attempt to understand the world within specific paradigms, as we discussed earlier. Again, think of the two thousand years it took for minds to be receptive for the rediscovery of the heliocentric worldview — initially developed by the Greek Aristarchus — by Kepler, Copernicus, and Galileo. Which is even more stunning when you realise that this worldview offers a much more logical explanation for astronomical observations than the geocentric model. It is because of these weaknesses that doubt, scepticism and an open scientific debate are so essential. This is not just in science: in society at large, truth has the highest chance of emerging from the competition of ideas in a free, transparent public discourse. It is also because of these weaknesses that Schopenhauer advocated restraint in education: better to acquaint children with the observable world first, before teaching them concepts, because without experience, the latter will be misapplied and cannot easily be adjusted.[93] In any case, experience is much more important for gaining understanding than knowledge. Therefore, as a rule, an experienced person tends to be wiser than a smart person, and wisdom comes with age, not with a high IQ. This explains why so few educated people have the common sense that uneducated people often do, as also Schopenhauer observed.[94]

Adam: The higher the education, the lower the common sense? This reminds me of a quote by George Orwell: 'There are some ideas so absurd that only an intellectual could believe them.'

Hugo: How true!

Adam: So, there are quite some flaws in our intellectual capacity. Not only is human knowledge limited in how far it can lead to philosophical understanding, but the mind is also not designed, sophisticated enough, or flexible enough to comprehend the complex world we live in.

Hugo: Indeed. Our intellectual capabilities are grossly overrated, especially when compared to the ingenious workings of other parts of the human body. As Schopenhauer wrote: everything brought about by means of the human intellect is nothing but botching and bungling compared to the physiological and biochemical processes brought about without that intellect.[95] Now you understand, Adam, how the intellect can so easily fool the human mind and satisfy its need for theories and explanations that promise heaven on earth with outlandish theories that are detached from common sense. Like socialism, a theory, in the words of American writer and economist Thomas Sowell, 'with a record of failure so blatant that only an intellectual could ignore or evade it.' But also in the aftermath of the horrors caused by these ideologies does the weakness of the human mind reveal itself. Once again, among all of the misery and atrocities that National Socialism caused, the Holocaust is undoubtedly the most repugnant. It remains mind-boggling that a people known for its poets, composers, and philosophers (including Schopenhauer!) could, in the course of just a few decades, become responsible for the destruction of a large part of Europe's Jewish community, a destruction carried out, moreover, in an unprecedentedly industrial and planned manner.

Adam: I'm glad you acknowledge that.

Hugo: But the problems start with determining *what* then the lessons are to be learned from this pitch-black period. For instance, some draw parallels between people criticising mass immigration on the one hand, and the rise of fascism and Nazi Germany on the other. Look at the way right-wing, populist parties are, especially in Europe, often associated with fascism and right-wing extremism. We know that one cause of the persecution of Jews in Nazi Germany was that they were made scapegoats for many problems facing Germany of the time, including a deep economic crisis. Now, people who associate right-wing parties with fascism and right-wing extremism argue that history is repeating itself in the form of similar sentiments towards other religious ethnic minorities, such as Muslims. Like the minority Jews then, they say, the minority Muslims now are held responsible for social problems and accused of lacking loyalty to the country where they live. In addition, both minorities suffer racist prejudice from the native, white majority. It is thus on the basis of these parallels that the attitude towards Jews before and during the war are compared to that towards contemporary minorities, and thus between right-wingers now, and the German Nazis of old. But this is where the tendency to over-abstract, overgeneralise and oversimplify rears its head: people often fall into easy explanations and theories by presenting things simpler than they are, or by making false generalisations or historical comparisons. Because why would being a religious or ethnic minority — a shared characteristic that forms the basis for the alleged parallels — be a relevant similarity? After all, there are significant differences between these two groups. Regardless of the causes, Muslims in Western Europe experience relatively high unemployment and are often overrepresented in crime rates. Jews in the 1930s were better integrated and economically more successful. Not to mention the fundamental religious and cultural differences between the two. There are also significant differences between the German of the early 20th century and the European of today who is concerned about Islam and mass immigration. The Germans then lived in a society that was culturally and economically a totally different one.

Adam: Drawing meaningful parallels between phenomena and collecting them under one concept requires identifying the right — that is, relevant — shared characteristics, and ignoring irrelevant, superficial similarities. Which is not done here, you say, referring to the weakness of the human intellect you mentioned earlier. The Jews of then are being unjustifiably compared to immigrants of today on the basis of irrelevant similarities?

Hugo: Exactly. With far-reaching consequences, as it practically leaves society powerless to deal with a very serious issue, namely mass migration.

Adam: But it is not only the left that draws unjustified parallels with World War II. The right also does this when it associates leftist politics with fascism on unreasonable grounds.

Hugo: That is absolutely true. Both left and right are guilty of this. I mentioned the example of minorities because it is so influential, and as a result we are left with a taboo on discussing a major social challenge. And so, the cause lies not so much in political opportunism (although this certainly also plays a role), but primarily in a fundamental weakness in our brain. Incidentally, the persistence of frames of mind also plays a role here. Once the idea has taken root that Muslims should be seen as the new Jews, or criticism of negative aspects of mass immigration or the Islamic faith should be interpreted as an expression of (latent) fascism, these frames of mind tend to be persistent and difficult to adjust.

Another consequence of this intellectual weakness is that it makes us susceptible to manipulation. Conservative author Jonah Goldberg claims in his book *Liberal Fascism*[96] that the associations of fascism with the extreme right — an important element of the dominant frame of mind discussed here — was deliberately brought into the world by Stalin. Goldberg argues that National Socialism was in fierce competition with communism in Germany in the 1930s. It was at that time Stalin himself who labelled National Socialism (and with it fascism) right-wing and conservative, the archenemy of left-progressive currents, with the intention to undermine its competitor. Which would make this one of communism's most successful propaganda campaigns, given the broad acceptance of this association to this day.

Adam: People's intellectual capacity is not as well developed as we generally assume. Funny, that's something you never think about, but explains a lot. This reminds me of another saying by Aldous Huxley: 'Man is so intelligent that he feels impelled to invent theories to account for what happens in the world. Unfortunately, he is not quite intelligent enough, in most cases, to find correct explanations. So that when he acts on his theories, he behaves very often like a lunatic.'

Hugo: But oh, how proud man is of this intellect, this intelligence that distinguishes him from animals! But Schopenhauer extensively refuted the haughty confidence in reason, this 'human delusion of grandeur', in the words of Schopenhauer's biographer Rüdiger Safranski, even before the dramatic effects made themselves felt.[97] Man is more animal than he cares to admit, more 'willing' than 'knowing' and thus more irrational than rational, with his intelligence, moreover, 'programmed for survival, not truth', as John Gray put it:[98] merely a trait to better survive in a world a lot simpler than the present one, let alone that his intelligence is equipped for the task it is deployed for by modern man. We have seen the dramatic consequences of this in the more than 150 years since Schopenhauer's death.

Adam: What you're saying is that people need to be taught that not only is the pursuit of utopias delusional and destined to end in nightmares, but also that the mind itself needs to be distrusted?

Hugo: Our mind is all too often a malfunctioning compass that steers us in the wrong direction. This is in addition to the fact that, as we have elaborately discussed, it rarely leads us to true insight into the nature of the world and of ourselves.

Adam: And what does this mean for politics in your view?

Hugo: Well, mainly, these intellectual limitations must be taken into account. Thus, in the field of political decision-making, common sense must be given a strong voice and influence to counterbalance a political elite that is all too susceptible to the fallacies of the intellect, and without correction can quickly transform into a detached, self-absorbed, and increasingly power-hungry globalist class. Into an 'aristocracy of brains', in the words of American sociologist Christopher Lasch,[99] characterised by tribal loyalties that can partly explain the contemporary unhealthy close ties between various branches in government, media, corporate life, and other institutions in society. This correction can take place peacefully by making decision-making as democratic as possible so that the people — often so much wiser than the educated class — can apply the brakes where necessary. However, the problem is that this elite, precisely on the basis of its supposed intellectual superiority, feels justified in curtailing this democracy (and the free debate associated with it) on the grounds that the public allegedly lacks the intellectual capacity to understand and deal with complex issues. Rather, the ruling class favours the opinions of 'experts' and technocrats, and prefers to place decision-making in the hands of often international institutions and treaties outside of democratic control. In their logic, it is inevitably the expert who should have the last word, and decision-making is best done in a top-down, centralised manner. Decisions moreover that often aim to transform society, inspired by the utopian thinking that we talked about earlier.

Adam: Or transform humans even, as we see in the transhumanism movement.

Hugo: Yes, transhumanism, where utopian thinking and intellectual hubris find each other in harmony! For some, the distrust of the people and the ambition to fundamentally change society even results in a belief in the blessings of a totalitarian state, in which the government controls and influences almost every facet of its citizens' lives, something that technological advances in information technology and artificial intelligence have made possible for the first time in history.

Adam: So totalitarian tendencies are not just grounded in a lust for power and control, see George Orwell's *1984*, or an extreme distrust or disdain for ordinary people, but can find utopian justifications as well.

Hugo: Indeed, especially when people see the totalitarian state as a means towards bringing utopian ideals of unity and equality to human societies (which, of course, will always be doomed to fail). As Aldous Huxley remarked,

> [...] the cult of unity on the political level is only an idolatrous *ersatz* for the genuine religion of unity on the personal and spiritual levels. Totalitarian regimes justify their existence by means of a philosophy of political monism, according to which the state is God on earth, unification under the heel of the divine state is salvation, and all means to such unification, however intrinsically wicked, are right and may be used without scruple.[100]

Adam: Still, with your talk of intellectual hubris and disdain for ordinary people, are you not yourself guilty of demonising a particular group, namely the elites? You mentioned communism and fascism. Let me then mention the reign of terror of the Cambodian Khmer Rouge in the 1970s, which exiled every educated person from cities and forced them to work in state-run farms in most appalling conditions, often resulting in death.

Hugo: Yes, I absolutely recognise the danger of demonisation. After all, it is human nature to look for too simple solutions and explanations, sometimes leading to the stigmatisation of a particular group in society — see Huxley's intellectual sins. Of course, I am by no means 'against' intellectuals. On the contrary, any society needs writers, doctors, scientists, and teachers — not to mention philosophers. What I mean to say is that every healthy society exhibits a good balance between the voices of the people and those of the elite, between individuals with low and high education, in order to counterbalance our intellectual hubris. As well as our other sins of course, such as greed and lust for power, which also are showing their ugly face in these times.

Adam: That all sounds very conservative.

Hugo: Because that's exactly what it is, Adam. Conservatism is the philosophy that distrusts reason and, in contrast, cites tradition, customs and institutions as sources of implicit (tacit) knowledge and wisdom, developed and adjusted over centuries in an organic process; a movement that realises that power corrupts and must therefore be scrupulously controlled, decentralised, and divided. But it is also a philosophy that acknowledges the value of individual freedom and autonomy, and recognises that not too much should be expected at the level of the state and politics. For the conservative, culture is much more important for a society: 'The central conservative truth is that it is culture, not politics, that determines the success of a society.'[101] Man therefore benefits more from religion than from politics. For religion is pre-eminently able to give man insight into his limitations, as well as into his deep, fundamental bond with his fellow man and the world around him; to lift 'man above himself and his temporary existence',[102] as Schopenhauer so beautifully put it, all essential elements for a firmly established morality and a stable society. Even more importantly, religion shows the only way to salvation, to 'the true and only heaven',[103] and can thereby at the same time save us from the fallacy of utopia. A salvation that can only be reached by the individual, never by society at large.

Adam: But what version of perennialism can accomplish this task, Hugo? What form should this message take to suit the needs and characteristics of modern man?

Hugo: That's a good question. As I said, I think Christianity is on its last legs. Even Gnosticism, in which the perennial philosophy is very purely expressed, has not been able to give a new impetus to this religion.

Adam: Perhaps Buddhism?

Hugo: As a doctrine whose central message is the imperfection of life, the illusory nature of the self, and the containment of desire — the will! — as a path to enlightenment, it is an almost ideal representative of perennialism. Moreover, Buddhism's strength is that it, focusing on the path to salvation, does not need to rely as much on metaphysics, which means it needs to lean less on myths and allegories, the Achilles heel of religions. Partly because of this, Schopenhauer preferred Buddhism to all other religions,[104] but the question is whether the Western mind is ripe for this faith. Can the message of self-denial match the needs of modern, comfort- and pleasure-oriented man at all? Doesn't he already live in a Brave New World where, like Buddha in his father's palace, he is too much surrounded by luxury and shielded from illness, old age, pain, and death? And in our technological society, have we become too far cut off and alienated from our nature to choose a spiritual path? If so, a spiritual rebirth will not happen until our civilisation has further crumbled or even perished, and we have had to experience our errors directly and at first-hand. But either way, we must hope that when that time comes, whether soon or in a few hundred years, the works of Schopenhauer and other representatives of the perennial philosophy will be available to germinate in the then fertile soil. For, to end with the Bible after all: the truth will set us free.[105]

References

1. Van Melsen (2004) *From Atomos to Atom*, Mineola, New York: Dover Publications, p. 11.
2. William James (1929) *The Varieties of Religious Experience*, New York: Longmans, Green and Co., p. 508.
3. Arthur Schopenhauer (1966) *The World as Will and Representation*, Mineola, New York: Dover Publications (volume II), p. 463. Further, this work will be cited as WWRI (volume I) or WWRII (volume II).
4. *Shankara's Crest-Jewel of Discrimination* (1970), Vedanta Society of Southern California.
5. For this and subsequent references to Huxley in this chapter, see the essay 'Knowledge and Understanding', in: Aldous Huxley (1992) *The Divine Within*, New York: Harper Perennial.
6. Elaine Pagels (1979) *The Gnostic Gospels*, London: Weidenfeld and Nicolson, p. XIX.
7. See for example, Sam Harris (2012) *Free Will*, New York: Simon & Schuster.
8. See for example the works of the Dutch neuroscientist Victor Lamme.
9. From Victor Lamme (2019) *De Vrije Wil Bestaat Niet* (Free Will Does Not Exist), Amsterdam: Prometheus.
10. Huxley, *The Divine Within*, p. 43.
11. WWRII, p. 198.
12. Huxley, *The Divine Within*, p. 43.
13. Ibid, p. 63.
14. WWRII, p. 201.
15. WWRI, p. 281.

16. See Arthur Koestler (1978) *Janus: A Summing Up*, London: Hutchinson & Co.
17. For example, WWRI, p. 281.
18. See for example, WWRII, pp. 4, 32.
19. WWRI, p. 3.
20. Arthur Koestler (1978) *Janus: A Summing Up*, London: Hutchinson & Co., p. 249.
21. See, for example, Lee Smolin (2007) *The Trouble with Physics: The Rise of String Theory, the Fall of a Science, and What Comes Next*, Boston: Mariner Books.
22. This chapter is an elaboration of the author's PhD thesis, available at jpvanrossum.com.
23. From Jacques Monod (1972) *Chance and Necessity: An Essay on the Natural Philosophy of Modern Biology*, New York: Vintage Books.
24. See *Chance and Necessity*.
25. See, for example, George C. Williams (1966) *Adaptation and Natural Selection*, Princeton: Princeton University Press; and Richard Dawkins (1976) *The Selfish Gene*, Oxford: Oxford University Press.
26. For a good overview, see Matt Ridley (1993) *The Red Queen: Sex and the Evolution of Human Nature*, New York: Perennial.
27. See Thomas Kuhn's influential 1962 work *The Structure of Scientific Revolutions*.
28. WWRII, pp. 642–643.
29. See, for example, WWRII, p. 195.
30. Sam Harris (2012) *Free Will*, Simon & Schuster.
31. Except at the level of quantum mechanics. However, this uncertainty provides no support for assuming free will, as Harris shows in *Free Will*.
32. See, for example, his *Essay on the Freedom of the Will*.
33. Arthur Schopenhauer (2005) *Essay on the Freedom of the Will*, Mineola, New York: Dover Publications, p. 98.
34. WWRII, p. 534.
35. From Giacomo Leopardi (1994) *The Canti*, Manchester: Carcanet Press.

36. Full title: *What Is Life? The Physical Aspect of the Living Cell* (1944).
37. See WWRI, p. 398 and onwards.
38. See his work *Janus: A Summing Up*.
39. See Philip Goff (2019) *Galileo's Error: Foundations for a New Science of Consciousness*, New York: Pantheon.
40. Arthur Koestler (1959) *The Sleepwalkers: A History of Man's Changing Vision of the Universe*, London: Hutchinson & Co., p. 339.
41. *Janus: A Summing Up*, pp. 224–225.
42. See, for example, 'Quantum Fields: The Real Building Blocks of the Universe, with David Tong': https://www.youtube.com/watch?v=zNVQfWC_evg (accessed July 2022).
43. From the 19th century play *The Tragedy of Man* by the Hungarian author Imre Madách (English edition by Corvina Kiadó, 1988).
44. See Huxley's essay 'Knowledge and Understanding'.
45. From his essay 'Additional Remarks on the Doctrine of the Suffering of the World', In: *Parerga and Paralipomena*, Part II (2015), Cambridge: Cambridge University Press.
46. WWRI, p. 324.
47. See his essay 'On the basis of morality'.
48. WWRI, p. 354.
49. 'That I recognise what holds the world together at its core'. From Goethe's *Faust*.
50. See WWRII, p. 640 vv.
51. Quentin Meillassoux (2014) *After Finitude: An Essay on the Necessity of Contingency*, London: Bloomsbury.
52. WWRI, p. 30.
53. WWRI, p. 5.
54. See, for example, WWRI, p. 28
55. Goff, *Galileo's Error*, p. 5.
56. See also Goff, *Galileo's Error*.
57. See Schopenhauer's essay 'Religion: A Dialogue', in *Parerga and Paralipomena*, part II. See also chapter 17 from WWRII.
58. Matthew 13:13.

59. Elaine Pagels (1979) *The Gnostic Gospels*, London: Weidenfeld and Nicolson.
60. Aldous Huxley, *The Divine Within*, p. 15.
61. Aldous Huxley (2004) *The Perennial Philosophy*, New York: Harper Perennial, p. vii.
62. F.C. Happold (1970) *Mysticism*, London: Penguin, p.20.
63. WWRII, p. 613.
64. WWRII, p. 605.
65. WWRI, p. 309.
66. Ecclesiastes 1:8.
67. *Parerga and Paralipomena*, part II, p. 228 (original sentence: 'falls upon every secure life in the manner of a lurking bird of prey').
68. WWRI, p. 379.
69. WWRII, p. 406.
70. John 12:25.
71. WWRII, p. 638.
72. Matthew 19:24.
73. Thomas à Kempis (2001) *De Navolging van Christus* (the imitation of Christ), Kalmthout/Utrecht: Pelckmans and Ten Have, p. 167 (translation by author).
74. Arthur Koestler (1945) *The Yogi and the Commissar*, New York: The Macmillan Company, p. 4.
75. WWRII, p. 610.
76. WWRII, p. 611.
77. WWRII, p. 560.
78. From his essay 'On the Sufferings of the World'.
79. WWRII, p. 640
80. From the poem 'To Count Carlo Pepoli'. In *The Canti* (1994), Manchester: Carcanet.
81. WWRII, p. 625.
82. From his essay 'On Religion', *Parerga and Paralipomena*, part II.
83. WWRII, p. 605.
84. *The Complete Works of Swami Vivekananda* (1963), Calcutta: Advaita Ashrama, volume 2, p. 65.
85. John Gray (2019) *Seven Types of Atheism*, London: Penguin Books, p. 1.

86. Aldous Huxley, *The Perennial Philosophy*, p. 251.

87. Jordan Peterson (2009) *12 Rules for Life: An Antidote to Chaos*, London: Penguin, p. 193.

88. Raymond Aron (2009) *The Opium of the Intellectuals*, New Jersey: Transaction Publishers, p. 266.

89. https://en.wikipedia.org/wiki/Mass_killings_under_communist_regimes (accessed July 2022).

90. 'This is not widespread knowledge.' Jordan Peterson on Soviet History: https://www.youtube.com/watch?v=XPfWThToClo (accessed July 2022).

91. From his essay 'On law and politics', in *Parerga and Paralipomena*, part II.

92. Ibid.

93. From his essay 'On Education', in *Parerga and Paralipomena*, part II.

94. Ibid.

95. WWRII, p. 269.

96. Jonah Goldberg (2008) *Liberal Fascism: The Secret History of the American Left, from Mussolini to the Politics of Meaning*, New York: Doubleday.

97. Rüdiger Safranski (1991) *Arthur Schopenhauer and the Wild Years of Philosophy*, Harvard: Harvard University Press.

98. 'The human mind is programmed for survival, not truth.' Gray, *Seven Types of Atheism*, p. 13.

99. See Christopher Lasch (1996) *The Revolt of the Elites and the Betrayal of Democracy*, New York: W.W. Norton & Company.

100. Aldous Huxley, *The Perennial Philosophy*, p. 11.

101. Quote from US politician Daniel Patrick Moynihan (1927–2003).

102. See WWRII, p. 167 (translation from German by author).

103. After the title of the book *The True and Only Heaven: Progress and Its Critics* by Christopher Lasch (1932–1994), in which the author criticises the idea of progress and argues for a moral conservatism.

104. WWRII, p. 169.

105. John 8:32.

Made in the USA
Monee, IL
18 September 2024

65479656R00098